DAMAGED

'People don't believe in heroes,
but they have not met my dad'

Chloe Stewart, Daughter

'Wish my former Spurs team-mate, Paul Stewart,
all the very best. Extremely courageous in telling his story'

Gary Lineker,
Spurs and England legend

'I hope he realises just how much his courage can help so
many other people. He was always a warrior on the pitch,
brave and strong – and now he is showing the same qualities
in a much more important fight'

Robbie Fowler, Liverpool legend

'When you look at what he went through,
you realise what a strong character he is'

Peter Reid, Everton legend,
former Sunderland manager

DAMAGED

DAMAGED

PAUL STEWART

Sport Media ⬤

'Your visions will become clear only when you can look into your own heart. Who looks outside, dreams; who looks inside, awakes'

C.G. Jung

This book is firstly dedicated to all the victims
who have suffered as I have over many years.
I hope it helps you in some way to come
to terms with your past. Always remember
that you are never alone.

Above all, I dedicate this book to
my wife Beverley and my three children
Adam, Chloe and Jade.
Words could not describe my love.

Paul Stewart

DAMAGED

Written with Jeremy Armstrong.

First published in Great Britain and Ireland in 2017 by
Trinity Mirror Sport Media, PO Box 48, Old Hall Street, Liverpool, L69 3EB.

www.tmsportmedia.com
@SportMediaTM

Trinity Mirror Sport Media is a part of Trinity Mirror plc.
One Canada Square, Canary Wharf, London, E15 5AP.

1

Hardback ISBN: 9781910335734
Trade paperback ISBN 9781910335819
eBook ISBN 9781911613022

Photographic acknowledgements:
Paul Stewart personal collection, Mirrorpix, PA, Blackpool Gazette.
Every effort has been made to trace copyright.
Any oversight will be rectified in future editions.

Jacket design: Rick Cooke.
Jacket image: Tony Woolliscroft.

Printed and bound by CPI Group (UK) Ltd, Croydon, CR0 4YY.

CONTENTS

Prologue: Paul Stewart   11
Introduction: Jeremy Armstrong   13

1.   I Do Not Know   19
2.   Day One   25
3.   Going Back   35
4.   Innocence Lost   45
5.   Manhunt   61
6.   Sound Of Silence   73
7.   Rebel With A Cause   85
8.   Mam And Dad's Story
     Every Parent's Nightmare   95
9.   Second Family   107
10. Look Back In Anger   123
11. Home Alone   137
12. On The Edge   155
13. Hero   159
14. Cocaine   169
15. Exiled   183

DAMAGED/CONTENTS

16.	Cold Turkey	199
17.	Turning Right	211
18.	Bev's Story *Tough Love*	223
19.	Survivors	235
20.	Justice	245
21.	A New Life	253
	Postscript: My Letter To A Victim	265
	What They Say	267

Prologue

CHANGING
A LIFE

I'll be honest. I thought I would take my secret to the grave. I never thought my true story would be told, let alone a book written about my life.

Before November 2016, you would have known me as Paul Stewart, former professional footballer. I played for Premier League teams and represented my country, sharing a pitch with some of the greatest players of my generation: talented superstars like Paul Gascoigne, Eric Cantona, Gary Lineker, Bryan Robson, Ian Rush and Roy Keane.

I can tell you funny stories about my life in football; anecdotes about Gazza, great days at Spurs with Lineker and El Tel. I can write about winning the FA Cup, the pinnacle of any player's career back then. I can tell you about the goals, the glory and the secrets of the dressing room.

But I'd be lying if I said this was the reason I was writing my book. I've never thought my football career warranted any sort of memoir, if I'm honest. My own personal view of my career is that I over-achieved. If you've picked up this book and you're looking to read a sportsman's autobiography then I'm afraid you will ultimately be disappointed.

That isn't the whole story.

So, who am I?

I am guessing that you have already read the headlines and seen press coverage of the ongoing football abuse investigation that has rocked our game.

My story will depict how the brutally desperate experience of being a young victim of sexual and physical abuse ripped me apart; turned me into a different person. I was someone who looked over the edge and stepped back to safety; someone who has gone about his everyday life as normal, despite a sense of desperation, anger, anxiety – even guilt – that has seeped into many an unfilled minute of my daily existence.

I have carried this secret throughout my life. Through my career – at Blackpool, Manchester City, Tottenham, England, Liverpool and beyond. My team-mates and managers never knew the *real me*. They knew the Paul Stewart who covered up things and blocked out the truth; they knew someone struggling to come to terms with the long-term impact of being a victim of child abuse.

My family were the same. One of the greatest gifts of being part of a family is that your wife, your children, your parents, your brothers know the *real you*. They know what drives you and understand the emotions inside that lead you to act the way you do.

Being a victim robbed me of that and worse, the ability to express my feelings towards those I love.

Then there are the fellow victims of abuse.

Many got in touch with me directly after I became front page news. The whole experience of going public made me realise how many people have suffered and are still coming to terms with the same hidden secret; how it has played on their minds throughout their lives, having an emotional impact on them, just like it has had on me.

This book is written for them as much as me. If it can help just one person to come to terms with the problems in their life, it has all been worthwhile.

Much has changed since the 1970s in terms of child protection in football. Since 2016, along with other victims, we have worked with the powers that be to put further preventative measures in place. What happened to me and other victims should never be allowed to happen again.

I deliberated long and hard about the title of this book because although I was 'damaged', the message is that you can come through and survive. I was damaged – not destroyed; I found a better place thanks to the help, support and love of other people. Talking to others is so important and I realise now how it has helped me deal with the secret which I carried for 41 years.

Paul Stewart, 2017

I first met Paul Stewart on November 25th, 2016, when he made the decision to tell the story of his childhood abuse to the world for the first time. Even before that first, remarkable encounter, his ability to laugh at himself came through.

He had sent an 'anonymous' e-mail to the *Daily Mirror*. But it came from an account which identified him as 'stewy10' and matched his Twitter and social media profiles. Our first telephone call began with the question: "Is that Paul Stewart by any chance?"

Despite the highly charged build-up to that first meeting, the natural nerves at what was about to unfold, Paul typically made a joke at his own expense. We were able to see a light side in the most difficult of circumstances. That would become a common theme in the coming weeks and months.

That first missive has taken us back to his darkest days; to his childhood home, now a dreadful reminder of the most horrendous ordeal overshadowing his happy, family life there.

To the former homes of his abuser and coach, Frank Roper.

To the places where Roper would take him to carry out his daily campaign of physical and mental torture.

To the spot where he took Paul, aged 11, the day the abuse began.

There are memories which will stay with me forever.

The playing fields of Paul's youth had an eerie silence with no teams there, not a soul in sight for miles around.

All those years later, it made me shudder to think how he had been targeted, how bewildered and lonely he must have been, an 11-year-old kid, alone with a trusted adult; I felt an anger towards Roper which would return time and again as his life story unfolded.

There were tears when I met Paul's mum and dad for the first time; good, hard-working people exploited and groomed just like their son. I felt the pain of his wife, brothers, children. They, too, were victims in all this.

Paul had carefully considered them in his decision to come forward, and that is typical of the man. He was to unlock secrets held all his adult life, from Roper's first knock on the front door of 28 Cleeve Road, Wythenshawe 41 years before. His first thoughts were for Bev, his wife of 29 years; his elderly parents Joyce and Bert – now 77 and 79, his children – son Adam and daughters Chloe and Jade – and his brothers Gary and Anthony.

Yet, his entire family was behind him from the off.

The details of that first interview were hard to bear but explained much of the behaviour, the legacy of the abuse – the drug addiction, the drinking – which they had seen at first hand for such a long time.

Paul's main concern was for them, especially Chloe, then pregnant with her first child, Sienna, born on March 1st, 2017.

Bev, who immediately gave her support for the decision, also expressed her pride at the courage needed to follow it through; if there had been any doubts, Paul may never have spoken. It was the love of the family which have brought him to where he is today – a changed man who has been through the hardest of times and come out the other side.

He had to tell Joyce and Bert news every mother and father dreads. Details of that terrible ordeal suffered by their little boy. There were tears and anger, unstinting support, steely strength amid the despair.

The same was true for his two brothers, Gary and Anthony.

They felt a sense of guilt shared by his parents.

Paul assured them all there was no way of knowing, all those years ago, what had happened in their midst, under their own roof.

There was only one person to blame. His name was Frank Roper.

What followed was an extraordinary few months. No one could have predicted the impact of the story.

That front page: '*England Ace: I Was Sexually Abused By Coach For Four Years*' was flashed on TV screens around the globe. Yet it triggered the reaction which Paul's selfless courage in waiving his anonymity so richly deserved.

Hundreds of other victims got in touch; with me, with Paul, with the police, with the FA, with the NSPCC. It became the biggest scandal to hit the game in modern history.

It was as shocking as it was unexpected; the sheer number of people who found the courage to say what had happened to them at football clubs, professional and amateur, up and down the land.

The personal details of his experience can only serve as a warning to others. But there was also, without question, an extraordinary sporting life, made all the more remarkable by what he had to overcome to make it.

Surely every amateur footballer to pull on a pair of boots has wondered what it is like to be in that changing room at Anfield, at White Hart Lane, at Old Trafford, as you prepare for action when Saturday comes. Everyone wonders what it is like to run out at Wembley for England. To score a goal in a cup final. To experience the incredible highs of victory before thousands of adoring fans, and the lows of defeats. Only those who have been there and done it can truly understand.

A young Paul also lived for months on end with Gazza, an enigma on and off the pitch, coming to terms with his world-wide fame post Italia 90, one of the greatest ever England players. There was the sheer madness of his antics. There were the funny stories which will make fans laugh out loud.

And yet, amid all these heady days with Spurs, Liverpool, and England, Paul was trying to tackle the demons of his past, the dreadful depression it caused, emotional turmoil and suicidal thoughts.

Many people these days equate money with happiness. Paul's experience of depression has shown that it does not matter if you are rich or poor; money does not cure it. Before he came forward for the first time, he was left to experience his trauma time and time again, alone.

I have come to understand that the trauma of abuse is so over-whelming, it shuts victims off from their feelings. That becomes a habit, and it is so hard to go back, to somehow repair the damage.

But Paul's story shows that you can find a way, with the help of family, friends, team-mates, and experts in the field. The dressing room may be a macho place, but even that is a support network; it makes you feel like you belong.

Paul Stewart has emerged from it all thanks to an incredible strength of character, and a courage rarely seen.

He is a credit to his family and the game he loves, and it is to his eternal credit that his motivation in telling this story has always been to help others. I feel privileged to be a small part of it, and to call him my friend.

Jeremy Armstrong, 2017

Chapter/1

I DO NOT KNOW

I am 11 years old, sat in the front of my football coach's car. He is angry.

He has just thrown the ball over my head and told me to go and fetch it. It's the second time he has done it. The first time I have done as he has asked. The second time, I know he has thrown it too high on purpose and it is a stupid thing to do, so I refuse. He is testing me, bullying me.

"What I say, you do!" he screams as we stand alone in a secluded spot on a vast playing field. He drags me by one arm and leads me back into his car. He is annoyed at my insolence.

"Right, get back in!" he shouts.

He opens the door and I slide in to the passenger seat.

I do not know then, but know now that I will see this car standing outside the school gates for years to come.

I can still see that red saloon with its shiny, silver headlights and the distinctive metal front grill. I can vividly recall the beige interior, powerful eight track stereo blasting out Jerry Lee Lewis and the Fiat badge on the black, glossy dashboard.

My coach is called Frank Roper. He is middle-aged and paunchy. He is in the multi-coloured *Umbro* tracksuit he always wears, though you could not meet a man who looks less like an athlete. He is unshaven. His wiry, dark hair is unkempt, as always.

A couple of hours earlier he has watched from the sidelines as I have played for my school football team.

He has given me and my dad a lift home after the school game and he has chatted in our living room. He has suggested I could do with extra training. Practice makes perfect. The more I practise, he says, the better my chance of becoming a professional footballer. The better the chance of making my dream come true. I am up for it. *My coach wants to give me extra training, he must think I am good.*

Before I know it, I am sitting in his car.

We are making the five-minute journey to the playing fields once used as the Manchester City training ground.

I do not know, cannot know, that I will go on to play for them one day. I do not know I will go on to play for England.

I do not understand that my coach, just a few days earlier, has already made the first calculated moves in an evil game.

"Who wants to drive?" he asked me and some of my team-mates cheerily after one training session. Of course we do. It is exciting behind the steering wheel. A glimpse into the grown-ups' world.

I am chosen and delighted to be the one picked. Yet when I have leaned over from the passenger side, with one leg over his lap and my hands on the wheel, I have felt his hand inside my shorts. I do not know what it means. Then suddenly his hand is gone. I forget it. Carry on as normal. *What else to do?*

Now, for the first time, I am alone with him in his car.

In the distance I can see the car lights on a busy road. They seem very far away.

I am wearing a training top. Underneath I am still wearing my school kit; blue and white checked shirt and the white shorts that we also use for P.E. I am wearing football boots that are hand-me-downs from our Gary with thick aluminium studs that you need pliers to pull out. It is a chilly late afternoon in October or November; the sky a deep, brooding Manchester grey.

We are tucked away, under the trees on a small car park where the ground is bare and worn from the heavy tyres of cars. We are far away from the safety of the dressing rooms and the little caretaker's house which sits like a tiny island on a sea of murky green. There are goalposts and pitches as far as the eye can see.

"What I say, you do!" my coach repeats, then from nowhere he slaps his hand hard across my face. It hurts. It is a shock.

The next 15 minutes or so are a blur. He leans towards me. I do not know what is happening. I feel a giant ball of fear well up inside my chest. My heart thumps and I am powerless to stop it. *What is going on?* I want to be at home. *Why is he being like this?* I want to be safe. I want to be anywhere except in this car on this gloomy, shadowy autumn afternoon. *Let me go.* I am trapped.

I sob uncontrollably, like I have never sobbed before; muffled yelps from the pit of my stomach. I cry for help. There is no one who can hear. No one who can come to my rescue.

When it is over, still the tears flow.

They will not stop.

My coach speaks. He does not raise his voice, but he speaks in a low, menacing tone that makes it clear that he means Every Single Word of what he says.

"If you say anything, I will kill your mam and your dad and your brothers. Do you understand?"

This is *The Threat*. Next comes *The Promise*.

"These are the things you need to do if you want to be a footballer…"

There is a brutal, empty silence.

Then, slowly, he mellows.

Still I am gripped by fear but his voice is no longer menacing. He needs to calm me down, stop me crying before he can take me home. Tears will only arouse suspicion at 28 Cleeve Road. *Why is your face red? Have you been crying? What have you been doing to my son?*

We stay in the car for what feels like half an hour, talking. At least *he* is talking. He mentions some new kit. Talks about the team. The games we are going to play, the exciting plans he has for my future.

Eventually, we drive home. As soon as the front door opens, I run up the stairs and into our bathroom. I turn on the taps and feel the hot water splash on my face. Then I go straight into my bedroom, shutting the door firmly behind me.

My coach has no such impulse to hide away. He accepts the invitation to join Mam and Dad in our living room. *The same people he has threatened to kill less than an hour ago.* I hear fuzzy voices, mingled in with the blare of the TV. I can only imagine the chat about the extra training, how Paul needs to practise more if he wants to realise his talent.

I DO NOT KNOW

I hear the goodbyes at the door as I lie on my bed, clutching the soft pillow to my cheek for comfort. I hear the engine start, and the car pulling away. He is gone. It is over. I shut everything from my mind. *Block it out.* Try to think only nice thoughts.

•••••••

The next day. 3.30pm. The bell sounds.

The doors burst open and at first a trickle, then a stream of smiling faces meander towards open arms and purring cars. The freedom of home time. What feels like a hundred happy voices fill the air; school is over for another day.

Freshly painted pictures and kit bags are thrust into parents' hands, hugs exchanged and sweets unwrapped. Teachers wave and friends shout their farewells. *Seeya!*

I trundle towards the school gates, my bag slung over my shoulder. Wandering through the crowds of parents, I suddenly hear a familiar voice.

"Jump in, Paul. We need to practise your close control today." I instantly recognise the ugly metal jaw and beady headlights of my coach's car.

"This is what you have to do if you want to be a footballer!"

I say nothing to him. I have nothing to say.

I do not know that I will be a star, that I will become what I have always wanted to be since my first days kicking a ball around the primary school yard: a professional footballer.

I do not know that this monster will abuse me every day for the next four years.

Chapter/2

DAY ONE

Friday, November 18, 2016

The day that would change my life started just as every other working day.

I own a business and our offices are a short drive from my home in Blackpool. A map of the world is behind my desk simply because I have businesses that cover as far afield as Australia and New Zealand, Canada and the USA. Also on the wall there is a big picture of Ryan Giggs holding aloft the Champions League trophy. Alongside Giggs is a signed canvas of Stevie Gerrard and Fernando Torres. We have a boardroom with various signed shirts and pictures, including Joe Hart and Eric Cantona. Sean Connery as James Bond stands by my office window – my business partner loves 007.

My BMW 7 Series is parked below. The offices are by no way plush but are adequate as they accommodate enough staff to service my businesses. I set up the company 14 years ago. I'm proud of what we've achieved.

Generally I get in early, before most arrive. I rise around 6am or 6.30am every day. I'm not a great sleeper, never have been. If I can get fours hours unbroken sleep, I'm happy enough. When it's early, it will be nice and quiet in the office and I can go through my e-mails without interruption. I must receive at least 100 overnight due to the time differences. After that, I would usually catch up on the day's news by reading the *Daily Mirror* online. The routine is the same today and with the emails read, I log on to the *Mirror*. A headline leaps out at me.

Coach who abused me was part of a football paedo ring

I jump to the top of the article and start reading; it tells the story of a former football player who has been subjected to child sexual abuse many years ago. I had never really heard of the player, Andy Woodward, but reading the article was like reading my own life story. There was something in Andy's account which hit a nerve.

> This will not be a total shock to some people within football. I'm convinced there's a lot more to come out. How many others are there? Only now I feel I can live without that secret, that horrible burden. I want to give people strength. We were victims in a profession where we were all so desperate to succeed...

There were very mixed feelings; all those disturbing memories from my own childhood were awakened. Andy, a former Crewe player, was the victim of a man operating at the heart of the junior Sunday League scene abusing children just as young as I had been, from the age of 11.

The story had a big impact on me. I started to hear a little voice inside. *You must tell your story. If you don't say something, this story will disappear and it will all be for nothing.*

DAY ONE

I read the article about three times, scrolling up and down, shifting in my chair, mulling over what actions I should take. Stan Ternent, Andy's manager at Bury, was one of the people he confided in. Ternent said: "It's been like a life sentence and he is so brave to put it out there."

The compulsion to come forward with my own story grew stronger. It was overwhelming. The more I thought about it, it felt right to speak out, not just in support of Andy, but in support of all the other victims of childhood abuse.

Then I was reminded of an awful truth. The terrible abuse I suffered every day for four years as a child between the ages of 11 to 15 was a secret I had carried alone for all these years. Not even Bev, my wife of nearly 30 years, knew about it.

That night, we were going to a *Simply Red* concert at Manchester Arena with Bev's twin sister Karen, and her husband Ian. I had decided that before I do anything I should really talk to Bev and also Ian and Karen about my plan to speak out, as we are a very close family. Bev and Karen are exceptionally close; identical twins, it's as if one knows what the other is thinking and feeling. Speaking to them was, of course, the right thing to do before going public.

I knew that my decision would impact on all our lives; my son Adam is 30 now, my youngest daughter Jade was 20 at the time, just about to turn 21; Chloe, now 27, was expecting her first baby, our first grandchild.

We were staying over in Manchester and the plan was to go to the hotel early that afternoon. I left the office early and headed home, sorting out our overnight bags before driving to the Marriott Hotel in Worsley. Manchester was busy that night and we couldn't get a place in the city centre.

I remember vividly the taxi ride from the hotel to the restaurant, where I planned to tell them the full story.

We were going to *San Carlo* in Manchester, which gets its fair share of celebrity diners. You will often see Manchester United and Manchester City footballers enjoying a meal there – along with pop stars. Noel Gallagher has been spotted at *San Carlo,* as have City players like Leroy Sané and Gabriel Jesus.

The taxi driver was talking about some of the VIPs he had taken to the restaurant and my brother-in-law was joking with him, saying: "It's not me that's famous, it's him…" pointing to me in the front seat, explaining that he did have a footballer in the car, but it was from a long time ago.

I tried to laugh along, join in the chat, but my heart wasn't in it. I had a lot on my mind.

Can we just get there? Can we just get there?

It felt as if I had the world on my shoulders. I was worried about the lifelong burden I was about to unload on them all.

I'd come a long way since the untold horrors of my childhood. I'd played for some of the biggest teams in the country; Manchester City, Tottenham, Liverpool. I'd fulfilled every boy's dream of lifting the FA Cup at Wembley. I'd played for England. And then I'd built a successful business. Through everything I'd carried this knowledge inside. Deep inside. The process of blocking it all out had made me a man I didn't want to be. I knew that the time had come to reveal everything; Andy's article had given me the chance I was looking for. But I was still anxious. How would I find the words?

We bought a bottle of white wine between us and made our menu choices. I was waiting for a moment to speak. It is my favourite restaurant, *San Carlo*, tucked away on the corner of a side street off Deansgate in the city; lavishly decorated with soft lighting and immaculate white table cloths with gleaming silver cutlery. But the wide open spaces with waiters scurrying between tables and people all around added to the tension; the difficulty of finding the right moment.

Then I plucked up courage and the fateful conversation began: "I want to tell you something…"

It all tumbled out in the end. There were questions, but mainly love and understanding. They told me to do what I had to do.

A secret that I had locked away and had kept from those I loved most, I was about to reveal and not just to my closest family, but to the nation, knowing that I would put myself in the spotlight again for the first time in many years – only this time, for very different reasons.

Bev had long suspected. From sheer instinct and female intuition, she knew something really serious had happened in my childhood. We'd never discussed it. It was hard to explain the need to do it now. It had taken all those years, almost all my adult life, to find a reason.

I had come close to making an admission in my late 30s. I was struggling with drink and drugs and my marriage was in difficulty. Bev had suffered enough of my mood swings; drinking and hangovers and I was staying with my parents for a few days – yet again. I confided in my mother about the abuse I had suffered. It came, as always, in drink.

My parents were in the bedroom next door, and I kept going in to see Mam, warning her: "I've got something important to tell you," then bottling out at the last minute.

After several attempts, I blurted it out. "Frank Roper abused me."

It was the middle of the night by then, and we both went back to bed. In the morning, in front of my dad, nothing more was said. But she had always assumed it had been physical, not sexual. The whole incident isn't something I remember.

On another occasion, my brother Anthony said I had blurted out something when I was a Spurs player, drunk outside a pub in Tottenham. Lots of things are said in drink. We were young. It wasn't brought up again.

I knew I had to tell my story now but the decision to go public still kept me awake at night. As well as my family, I thought about the impact it would have on other people I knew, such as the near 200 people working for my company.

Those closest to me knew it would be hard for all of us, that there would be people who pointed the finger about why I had done it, which is all part of being a public figure.

It had been a very difficult decision, a choice no one should have to make. But I knew it was the right thing to do.

Above all else, I owed my family.

•••••••

I was tentative about the approach to the *Daily Mirror* for obvious reasons. It was a journey into the unknown, uncovering the deepest secrets of my past.

But there was humour even in this, the most difficult of circumstances. I was cautious so I signed off anonymously as '*a troubled individual*' but I wrote the e-mail without thinking that my name would be included in the address line. It included not only Paul Stewart, but it was followed by 10 – my old shirt number. It didn't take a genius to work out it was me.

I am contacting you after reading your article about Andy Woodward in Friday's edition of the Daily Mirror. I am struggling on where to begin really, as you will notice I have omitted my name at this point, not because I am in any way embarrassed but because I know that this story needs to be investigated well beyond just a newspaper article.

What I can tell you at this stage is that I am an ex-England international who has played at every level for his country, and four major Premiership clubs.

I am contacting you today as I wanted to speak with my family over the weekend after Friday's article, to make sure they are comfortable with me telling my story, should you decide to print it, then it will have an effect on them.

I briefly outlined the abuse I had endured from 11 to 15 and revealed that I had contemplated suicide on many occasions — sometimes at the height of my playing career — and how I still sometimes went into very dark places. I talked about the impact my abuse had on the decisions I made later in life.

I have been addicted to class A drugs where I had to seek professional help. I turned to alcohol as a means to escape the constant mental issues that still haunt me.

The hardest part was trying to explain the emotional impact, how I found it hard to express my feelings, my deeply felt love even for my wife and children, which had caused such upheaval within my family down the years.

I know now how lucky I am that they have stood by me,
considering all my issues, but I know that they have just
learned to live with it, and understand me.

And, of course, it was not just about me.

There was not just the impact on my life; I knew there were many other victims of my abuser. There were so many former young players, now adults, who did not make it professionally but had endured the same ordeal.

Two still lived close to me. I told the newspaper that I would not name them, but that I would name the abusers in the ring linked to the paedophile who had abused me for four years. I named a former Premier League club scout with links to him. Both men scouted for many clubs, and had a reputation for spotting young talent and taking that talent to some of the biggest clubs in the North West. The last man was a former manager. It came to me then, for the first time, that this was a story which went far beyond my own, and would have implications for our national game.

The interview, when it came four days later, was a release.

I had bottled up the secret of my abuse for 41 years and it was somehow right that I told the story now. I wanted to support the players who had come forward – most notably Woodward – but above all to give those other victims out there the strength to speak out.

I told of my suffering at the hands of my former coach Frank Roper, how he threatened to kill members of my family if I ever told anyone about his crimes; how he had abused me every day for four years – and yet somehow got away with it. I had to waive my right to anonymity, but my family's support, the fact that my wife, children, parents, brothers, even my elderly aunts and uncles and extended family had all stood by me gave me courage.

The shocking truth was that Roper had threatened to kill both my mum and dad, and my brothers, if I ever spoke a word to anyone about what he did. There was high emotion, and tears at times because of the impact of the abuse. It was devastating for that all to be laid bare.

Even in the TV interviews afterwards – and there were many, as I made the decision to get the message out there as much as I could – that was always the hardest aspect of the abuse. Its impact on my kids, my loved ones, my entire family, my inability to say quite simply what I felt.

It became apparent in doing the *Mirror* story just how much I had learned to block out details of the abuse, and all those memories. The hardest part was the obvious – just how young I was. Still at primary school, I had only just turned 11 when it all began, and in truth I was so young that I did not even know what was happening at first.

That first interview, published on the front page and over four pages inside of the *Daily Mirror*, stirred up a past which I thought I had long buried. I awoke on November 23rd, 2016 to the headline:

England ace: I was sexually abused by my coach for four years

It was, in fact, the first day of the rest of my life, the first day when everyone knew of my past.

Chapter/3

GOING BACK

To understand my story, I need to take you back to the start.

I returned to 28 Cleeve Road, Wythenshawe, for the first time in many years while writing this book. It was a chilly March day as I headed on the motorway one Tuesday morning towards Manchester. My childhood home is only about 50 miles from my house in Blackpool yet I haven't felt the need to return. My family moved away from the area 18 or so years ago and there's nothing to bring me back to these parts anymore, except memories.

I wasn't sure what I'd feel as I turned off the M60 and drove along the roads that were once so familiar to me. Fell Park Road, Southwick Road, Brent Road.

Pulling up alongside our old house, I think that nothing much has changed. The little strip of green to the front is still there, though it seems much smaller now. As a kid it seemed massive, our own sacred patch of grass, on which we would live out our football fantasies. The 'No Ball Games' sign which we used to ignore as kids is gone.

When I was older, I built a fence around the garden. I was so proud showing my parents when they came in from work. It was built to keep the ball in.

No doubt Fred is gone too. Fred was the neighbour who lived opposite as I was growing up. A mere mention of his name is enough to bring a knowing smile to the face of our Gary, one of my older brothers. We regularly put Fred's windows out with the ball. It didn't stop us playing because Fred never complained. He was too afraid of my dad to do that.

Dad is 79 now. Herbert – or Bert as he is known – was a labourer when he was in work. He couldn't read or write but still managed to scribble the number of a horse on a betting slip at the bookies. He gained a bit of a reputation as a lad in his younger days. Got barred from a few pubs for fighting, so the story goes. He certainly stood no messing around when we were kids. He taught us to fight our own battles. And he made sure we went to bed on time every night. You didn't argue, otherwise you could get Mam's slipper which could hurt if you didn't make it out of the door in time.

My mother, Joyce, always 'Mam' to us, worked most of her life at a textile factory in Wythenshawe on a production line folding ladies garments. Mam is 77 now. She was a real driving force in the family. I always remember she used to tell me: "There's no such thing as can't!" When I was struggling with injuries at the end of my career she reminded me of that. Mam and Dad are coming up to their 60th anniversary now which is a credit to them.

I have two brothers. Gary is exactly three years older than me – we share the same birthday, October 7 – while Anthony is five years my senior. When I think about it now, I am very lucky to be called Paul. I could be standing here now called something very different. When Mam was pregnant with me in the summer of 1964, the Beatles were at the height of their fame and my two brothers wanted to name me after one of the band. Unfortunately for me it wasn't John or Paul or even George, they wanted Mam to call me Ringo. Luckily, common-sense prevailed, and I was duly named Paul after Sir Paul McCartney!

I was above average size as a youngster, quite skinny with a mop of curly brown hair and a distinctive gap in my front top two teeth. I was actually born in a tiny council flat not far from here. A request by Mam and Dad to the council got us a smart pebble-dash new house which boasted a garden front and back, living room, kitchen, small dining room, bathroom and outside loo, which I'm sure has long since been knocked down. Mine and my brother's bedroom was overlooking the back garden, which was usually overgrown. Most of our furniture would be second-hand or given to us by other family members and the multi-coloured carpet was well worn.

Mam recalls how I was one of the happiest children you could meet during my formative years.

We had a microphone and a tape recorder in the house and I would sing songs for her and 'make my own records' so she could listen to them when she got in from work. There was a terrible rendition of *Bohemian Rhapsody* by Queen which must have been when I was around 11. She treasured it. Many years later, the family car was stolen and all she could say to Dad was 'it had Paul's tape in.'

When there were special birthdays and christenings, Mam always says that I would always be laughing and messing around. My cousins called me *Paulee Doo*, as I was game for anything. They would always dare me to do things, and I would always go through with whatever they wanted me to.

Not far from here would be the ABC Cinema. It's a Jehovah's Witness meeting place now. Growing up I would go to the ABC Minors – the Saturday morning kids club. I might sneak in just in time to hear the song which started the show: *'We are the boys and girls well known as Minors of the ABC...And every Saturday we line up...To see the films we like and shout aloud with glee...'*

I loved any films with James Cagney in, *Angels With Dirty Faces* being my all-time favourite. I loved telly too. I'd curl up and watch *Blue Peter* and *How*. If I was lucky, I might be watching with a 2p lucky bag on my knee, containing some sweets and a toy. Or a piece of bread toasted in the coal fire. I loved any programme to do with sport. *Grandstand, Kick-Off* on Friday night and *Match of the Day* on Saturday if you were lucky. On Sunday afternoons, I'd watch more footy highlights. I vividly remember Frank Worthington's wonder goal for Bolton when he juggled the ball before flicking it over his head and hitting it on the volley into the corner of the net.

I'd usually be playing outside any chance I got and if I didn't have a football at my feet, I might be riding my bike. I only remember being bought one bike, I think it was for my eighth or ninth birthday. It was the time when *Choppers* and *Tomahawks* were all the rage.

I desperately wanted a racing bike to be able to race the other lads off the estate. I knew we couldn't afford a new one, but my parents looked in the *Manchester Evening News* for a second hand one. We went to a house, and there was one bike they could afford. It was a green *Chopper* but the handlebars had been broken, so somehow the fella selling it to us had attached old rusty racing bike handlebars. But it was on sale for a tenner, if that, so I ended up with this peculiar looking bike that my parents convinced me was perfect as it would be ideal to get me used to riding before they bought me a proper racing bike.

I never got a real racer, but to be honest, I loved the *Chopper* even if the lads on the estate took the mickey out of me. We used to race on our bikes around the block as we called it, as the estate was surrounded by a road.

For our summer holidays, we would go to Rhyl or Tenby in Wales. We would go by coach usually, unless one of our uncles took us in his car. I remember the coach journeys lasting for hours with endless pick-ups en route then the excitement of arriving at our caravan and playing in the fresh air with my cousins. We did have one holiday abroad when we went to Lloret De Mar on the Costa Brava but unfortunately we were all ill from the food and from swimming in the sea. I can't recall many trips with school but I do remember our Gary coming back with a broken arm when he went to France. He had stuck his arm out of the window when another train was passing!

My older brother Anthony was involved in another family drama that I remember. We were sat in the house one evening and there was a knock at the door. When my mam or dad answered it, there was no one there, but a brown parcel was left on the step. Just as one of them were about to open it, Mam or Dad said: "Watch out it could be a bomb!" It must have been around the time of the Troubles in Northern Ireland.

There was a panic and the police were called. The whole neighbourhood around 28 Cleeve Road was evacuated and the bomb squad was called in.

Then, as casual as anything, Anthony rocks up back from his mate's house and announces that the suspect package in fact contained leaflets. He had applied for a job out of the paper and had to post them through letter boxes. We have laughed about it for years, especially as one of the older neighbours kept tapping the package with his walking stick and saying: "It's ticking…" But his other hand was close to his ear as he was listening. It was his wristwatch that was ticking!

•••••••

As I drive along Cleeve Road on to Sale Road and then turn on to Yew Tree Lane, I can see the building that used to be the Yew Tree pub. Next to it, at one stage, there used to be a nightclub called 'Yewtopia'.

There used to be a butty shop close by, which was run by my mam and auntie when I first signed for Manchester City. It is in a circular parade of shops which are still there to this day. It became quite famous locally. I used to come back after training with City and have a butty and there would be kids looking for autographs.

As you'd expect, there was massive rivalry in the city between City and United. Even our family was split. I followed our Gary in supporting United. Anthony supported City. My Dad was also on the red side in those days, though now he's a City fan.

I must have been seven or eight years old when I first went to see United in the Stretford End Paddock with Gary. The likes of Joe Jordan, Lou Macari and Martin Buchan were my heroes. When England played, it would be Kevin Keegan. We'd go as often as we could to Old Trafford, but we didn't always have enough for the bus fair and a ticket. I can still recall the sights and sounds of the stadium on a matchday. And I vividly remember the smell of winter green, an ointment the players rubbed on their legs when it was cold. I remember my first professional game for Tottenham, and the smell was exactly as I remembered, especially when both teams were stood in the tunnel waiting to go out. That took me back.

As early as I can remember, right back to primary school days, I knew that I wanted to be a footballer. As a working class kid on a council estate in Manchester you either played football or you didn't fit in with the rest of the 'gang', the lads who lived around the area.

I used to play every hour God sent on the green by our house, the back fields, the park, anywhere there was a bit of land where a group of lads could get a game on. If it was a good day, we'd be playing with a *Wembley Trophy*, the distinctive orange ball with black pin-stripes. I can almost hear now the hollow twang of ball on concrete. The *Trophy* was better than the cheaper flyaways which would always burst. We'd carrying on playing if they went flat, it was better than nothing. If we didn't have a ball, we'd kick a can around.

On Sundays we would play out all day. If there was enough off the estate, we'd have a big game or if not, we would play *Wembley* which was a knockout game, round after round of first one goal and then two until you got to the final. The loser always ended up in nets.

Often, in primary school days, it would be just me and Gary; Anthony would come along as well until he reached 16 and started work as a printer. I would follow Gary everywhere as he was my idol when I was growing up, a very talented player who I believe – I always say this to him – was a far better player than me.

But I could hold my own when I was playing with my brother and his mates. That was when I realised I was half decent at football. My talent was encouraged at school.

My old primary school, Rack House, is still there. It's about a ten minute walk from Cleeve Road. My secondary school, Yew Tree High School, is long gone and has now been replaced by a very modern site for Manchester College. But the sports fields are still there. The fields that hold a lifetime's significance to me now, for such unhappy reasons, as you will learn.

At school, I was always made captain. Not just for football, for any sports. The teachers obviously saw something in me. I started as a midfielder in the school team when I was eight, even though most of the other players were three years older than me. I got moved up front when I was 11. That's when I started playing for the city team.

Manchester Boys played at a place called Mersey Bank, it's near Southern Cemetery off Princess Parkway, the road that leads to Manchester City's old ground, Maine Road. All the age groups played there. The kit was royal blue shirts, shorts and socks. It was an exciting time.

Coming back to Cleeve Road all these years later I can see in my mind's eye that I was just a carefree, normal kid in a typical family. I can look back at the lad I was and smile.

Those early days were happy and I was happiest of all when I had a ball at my feet. I went on to achieve a lot in the game – though I always say that I over-achieved – but I'm not sure the buzz I got from pulling on an England shirt was much different from the innocent thrill of scoring the winner in a kick-around with my brothers and mates on a sunny summer's day on a Sunday afternoon.

I'm 52 now, lucky enough to afford a decent car. I'll treat myself to the odd pair of *Gucci* shoes and a *Burberry* coat now and then. When I was a young lad growing up I didn't get footy shirts or fancy football boots. It was all very different. We came from a relatively poor family. When someone turned up offering you those things – *adidas* boots, fancy sports gear or whatever – then your eyes lit up. Why wouldn't they?

As I start the car and head back to Blackpool, leaving my old life behind, I think to myself that I suppose I'm proud I made it as a professional footballer. From this little patch of Cleeve Road turf to Maine Road, White Hart Lane, Anfield, Wembley...so many fall by the wayside but I did it.

Yet nobody knows the price I had to pay. Nobody knows the desperation behind every step I took up the ladder.

Nobody knows my secret.

I used to collect *Panini* footy stickers as a kid. I would take my swaps into school and exchange them with my mates. There was always one player which was harder to get. For some, you had to hand over three cards to get the one you wanted. I always remember looking at my sticker book and as clear as anything I could remember thinking: *I'm going to be in this book one day.* Being a footballer was my dream.

Following that dream as a young lad would lead me down a road from which there was no return.

Chapter/4

INNOCENCE LOST

After that first terrifying episode of sexual and physical abuse in his car, it became obvious that this would become a daily routine. And every time it happened, the more I withdrew into myself. I was paralysed. I didn't know what was happening and the threats to my family made me feel very alone. I thought maybe this was really what I had to do if I wanted to be a professional footballer.

Roper had taken his first steps into forbidden territory when he touched me as I sat on his lap while driving his car. I could only have known him for a matter of weeks when this happened and it could only have been a day or so later when he started an inappropriate conversation that clearly pointed towards his sick intentions.

He used to give a few of us a lift home after training and I always seemed to be the last one to be dropped off. With the two of us alone in the car, he asked me: "How often have you masturbated today?" It immediately felt wrong. I said anything just to avoid dealing with the situation, blurting out: "Once, twice, three times…dunno…!" He wasn't threatening the way he asked, but he insisted on an answer.

At the time, of course, I didn't think it would lead to something serious. In hindsight now, four decades later, I can see that this was the next step in the process. No doubt he would be monitoring my reaction and building up a picture of how I would react if he performed a sexual act on me – as he did that night in the playing field car park.

Roper had first approached my dad Bert at a school game very near to my house. *Who's the dad of the number 11? Who's the dad of the number 11?* He walked up and down the touch-line asking the parents.

Some time later I heard the brass knocker go on our door sending a dull thud throughout our house and I heard Mam chatting to someone. It was him.

"'I'm Frank Roper, I run a Sunday morning team called Nova Juniors. Your Paul's a good player. Would he like to join our team?"

I was buzzing when I heard that. Nova were a top class local junior side with a big reputation and it was exciting to think they could be interested in me.

They were basically an unofficial feeder team to the big clubs. If you played for Nova, you had a chance of catching the eye of one of the scouts who regularly patrolled the touch-line during our games. During the time I played, Nova would help numerous players get on the professional ladder. David Bardsley was a Manchester kid like me who played for Nova and went on to win caps for England. Then there was Derek

Hall (Coventry City), Steve Kennedy (Burnley) and Stuart Thompson (Rochdale).

"Would it cost anything?" asked Mam.

Money was tight and any extra pressure on the household budget might have been a problem. But when Roper assured her that it would cost nothing, she agreed. Why wouldn't she? I loved playing football and here was someone who was going to give me that chance to play even more than I was already, and at a more competitive level. It would help me get better.

By then, I was playing not only for the school, but representing the city. My loving parents did everything to support me with my football. One of them would watch me play in every game which in those days was pretty unheard of. Back then, it wasn't the thing to take time off work just to watch your kids play, not like today when you see an army of parents clutching juice bottles and coats and cheering on their sons and daughters.

When Roper first approached Mam and Dad, I was still at Rackhouse Primary school. So I had just turned 11 – I may even have been 10, as my 11th birthday came in October of 1975. My mam had no way of knowing that the decision to let me play would change the rest of my life. In fact, I had already told her I wanted to join Nova as I'd heard they were going on tour to America that summer.

Roper was embarking on a plan to charm and woo my entire family, as he moved into a position to groom me. He would have known – it was plain for all to see, even at under-11 school games – that I was desperate to be a footballer. And that was all he needed to know. It meant I found myself in that red 132 Fiat saloon time and again.

It was at the school gates when I left at home time, waiting, or it would follow me along the road before he picked me up. We were always sat in the front, as sitting with me in the back would have looked strange, even from a distance.

The mere sight of that car turned my stomach. I was an 11-year-old, lost and bewildered by this situation which I did not understand, thinking: *Oh no, here we go again.* The thought often came: *How do I get out of this?* I would say to my mother: "I want to give it a miss today, Mam" or "do you mind if we do it some other time?"

But she thought, as all my family did, that Roper was going to help me become a footballer; that I was just being lazy, wanting to skip training. And he just would not give up, stood there in his tracksuit, telling me: "Heading today, Paul" or "let's get down to the park to do some shooting practice."

••••••••

There were certain places Roper would go to make sure there was no chance of being caught. At first, he would always take me to the old Manchester City training ground. Then he progressed to different locations such as sheltered corners of a local park or the hushed darkness of a nearby athletics ground.

When I go back to the old City training ground now, I can see how it was the ideal location.

Stood on the motorway bridge looking out across the vast open spaces, you are hit by the emptiness of it; all those football pitches, as far as the eye can see, with a few trees scattered in between. There must be more than a dozen used by local teams.

To any onlooker, a passer by, dog walker, jogger, we would

have been tiny dots on the landscape, like a father and son playing an innocent game of footy.

No one ever knew the truth behind that scene, what would happen in the red car, always parked nearby.

People think *there must have been someone around* when he got me. But there was never anyone around because he knew how and where to do it. He must have built up a mental image and timetable of the local area. The comings and goings of groundsmen, park gardeners and local bobbies on the beat must have been factored into his thinking as he schemed and planned out prime locations to indulge his warped fantasies.

Roper was precise and careful. Sly. He had abused countless times before with other boys, and as I would discover, he would do it again for years after me – in the UK, at tournaments in Ireland, America, and when he lived in Thailand in later life, by that time in his 60s. He got away with it all his adult life, stretching over decades, from the '70s to the '90s.

Roper would be rapping the door knocker if he missed me at the school gate or couldn't find me nearby. Often, we'd head to the athletics stadium at 'Wythy Park', as we called Wythen-shawe Park.

Images still flash by in my mind's eye of those journeys to hell: I am in the front seat, looking out on Orton Road, close to my primary school, past the landmark Yew Tree pub and through the middle of our typical 1970s council estate with its neat rows of semis, gardens front and back. Then the muddy road to the car park and the athletics track. There was no gate, as there is now, to stop the cars after dark. I was trapped.

It was always the same routine; darkness would fall and that terrible empty silence descended, as the full horror dawned of what was about to happen to me. The other kids would all disappear from the athletics track, the car park, the grounds. Then came that doom-laden walk back to the car.

I would think: *We are all alone, again.*

He would force me to commit acts on him, or him on me. I could not wait for it to be over, to get home.

On other occasions, he would take me to his Stockport home, a new-build, where my mother and other mums would later give up their time to pack sports tops to raise money for the trips abroad.

I can vividly recall the car pulling up outside the property, a neat, Barratt Homes-style modern semi-detached house on an estate full of them; nothing flash, nothing out of the ordinary, just like Roper himself.

We would often go to his mother's house nearby first.

There I would be, a little boy afraid of what was coming next, sat outside the old Roper family home in his car, still in my football kit, boots and top. I suppose the neighbours must have seen me but why would they have thought anything was amiss? Roper ran a local junior football team and I was just one of the players. *Nice fella, Frank. Doing his bit for the kids in the area. He even gives them a lift to games.* If only they had known.

I never went in to his mum's house. You wonder now if that was deliberate. Would his mother have suspected something? Did she harbour doubts about her own son? Roper took no chances; I will never know now if that is why he kept me away from everyone who knew him well. It was just another trick to keep his cover; another means of hiding his true self.

Throughout this time, Roper used cruel mental tricks and bullying techniques to ensure he stayed in control.

INNOCENCE LOST

He would often be following me in his car after school, checking if I was talking to any other kids. If I was, even though that was completely normal for a child of that age, I would later get a back-hander. *Haven't I warned you about talking to him?* It was all part of the control, the mind games. It shocked me and made me think that I was doing wrong. I became paranoid. Even if my mates were just catching up to say 'hello' I was unsure about what I should do. Sometimes I shunned them. They must have thought I was strange. *What's up with Paul?* But I just didn't know what to do. I felt like I was being watched by Roper.

There were times growing up when we were so hard up that I would put the cardboard from a cereal box inside my shoe if the sole wore down. We would cut it to the shape of the insole and slot it inside. Of course, before too long, it would come away.

Look at how you are dressed, they can't love you. Roper would try to turn me against my own family. I was being brainwashed. His mind games left me confused, and I fell silent, trying to work out in my head all the time: *What can I do?*

Sometimes he would give me a forearm smash, sticking out his left hand so his arm hit my face as he drove the Fiat home, or hit me if I said something nice about my parents, or brothers as any innocent kid in a loving family would naturally do.

Any sign of rebellion was instantly punished. If I gave him some back-chat he might bend back my fingers, his big hand clutching mine, making me wince and screw up my face. That kind of physical cruelty was ideal because it hurt me but didn't leave a mark.

Even if he did hit me, he made sure he never damaged my

face. A few marks on my arms and legs were acceptable. Back in those days, it was not that unusual to come in with a few bumps and bruises from playing football or falling off your bike. It was all part of growing up.

If he ever thought I was confronting him, that's when I would receive the most severe treatment. He would beat me in that isolated car park by the athletics track. Slaps and punches raining in on me as I lifted my leg and covered my head with my arms for protection.

The physical and sexual abuse went hand in hand. There never seemed any pattern as to what order it happened. I never really knew what was coming next, whether I was going to be hit first and then abused or just abused.

I suppose above everything, the biggest shock was how frequently it all happened. When I say I was abused every day over the course of four years, it is no exaggeration. It does seem extraordinary, I know. But it is true. If there was the odd day he missed, they are not ones I can remember. School days, weekends, school holidays; rain or shine. It was a daily ritual.

This slowly dawned on me over that first year. The first encounter happened in the late autumn; the busy hum of Christmas came and went; the greyness of winter slowly turned to the bright colours of spring and day in, day out, there was the car by the school gate; the trips to the training ground and the athletics stadium. He was not going to go away.

Looking back now, I can see that not only was Roper a paedophile, but he was a paedophile with an insatiable appetite for abuse. A monster in every sense of the word.

I had no idea when it would stop. So I had to get on with life, focussing on football, thinking about my big chance.

I coped with things the only way I knew how, by putting up and shutting up. I built up a resistance to it, so that when I saw him at the school gates, I accepted it. If he was not there, I knew he would find me anyway. There was no escape.

The unspeakable acts were locked away in mind as a means of dealing with the trauma.

Going back to see his old haunts as I did for the first time in all those years did not upset me or make me break down, because that would have meant he still had control over me. I cannot let him have that effect on my life now. That would mean he has won.

•••••••

Roper was not the archetypal paedophile; he was not like the child catcher in *Chitty Chitty Bang Bang*.

I've already described him. He was not a good looking man in any way; he was never clean shaven, his hair was always scruffy. His secret was his apparent 'normality'. There was no tell-tale sign when others were there – there was never anything to make parents think he was anything other than 'Mr Average'.

He told me once that he nearly married after leaving the Merchant Navy, but he got a 'Dear John' letter.

Even now, all these years later, I find that hard to believe. A sister was mentioned, but I never met his family. He could not risk that.

By the time I reached 13, his sports business started to take off, so he stopped working as a photographer. Roper was buying gear direct from warehouses – there was an *Umbro* place nearby, and *Admiral*. Initially, he would have a market stall in local markets – my granddad helped out on one of them – then he got himself a shop in Manchester, and another one in Blackpool. He must have been pulling in huge sums of money as things took off. He used the parents from the Nova teams – Mam and Dad included – to sell his stock to friends, relatives and neighbours. He knew no shame.

Blackpool was busy because he was also helping to bring kids to the club for trials, and he provided gear directly to the club. The outlet in Cheetham Hill, not that far from his house in Stockport, was the same, turning over huge sums of money.

Roper was highly thought of at Blackpool Football Club because he was bringing them talented young players. It meant that he grew more ambitious in his means of gaining access to young children like me, including setting up trips abroad.

Shortly after I joined Nova, he set up an exchange with a US junior club in Boston, Massachusetts. I knew about a trip to the States before I had even joined and it excited to me to think that I could be joining a local club that toured faraway places.

Nova had three trips to America. The first trip was to Boston during that first summer. We went back a year later and started at Boston but then travelled around. The third time, when I was 14, we went to Anaheim, California. The trips to America were usually six weeks long. It was a long time to be away from home at that age.

On that first trip to Boston, there was a family who got really attached to me. Ed and Doreen were brilliant hosts, they could not do enough for their young English guests; taken by the accents, keen to show the best of their country.

They had a son of their own – he played for the opposition team – and they loved having an English kid in their home.

INNOCENCE LOST

They would ask me questions about Manchester, football, life in England, how I got on at school, my brothers back home. They loved to hear about every single aspect of life in Manchester. It was a big thing for them having someone to stay for the entire summer. I remember they bought me a baseball cap and a bat.

You could not have asked for more, and I loved it there; for whatever reason they were really taking a shine to me too. It felt good spending time with people like that.

All that ended as soon as Roper realised they were growing fond of me; he was losing control and he had to get me back as his possession. So he requested I move to a 'new' family for some spurious reason. Even then I was thinking: *That bastard has got me moved.* He always knew how to manipulate situations to his own advantage.

On all the trips, Roper always made sure he was in the same host family as me. On the second USA visit, we stayed at a politician's house, I think he may even have been a senator.

I remember driving up the mile-long driveway with my mind in a spin. *Look at this.* It was a window to another world. It meant I saw for the first time what money could get you. We had to stay in a certain wing of the property – Roper was still in the same bedroom as me.

You can imagine his pathetic excuses to the hosts. *He's only little. He gets a bit homesick. I told his folks I would look after him.* So, sharing a room with a middle-aged man was never questioned, despite the size of the house.

There were tennis courts, horses, a swimming pool, it was a big property somewhere close to Boston. It was hard to take in how luxurious it was, especially at that age. They were a typical American family, very friendly and hospitable, their son playing in the opposition team. They had money beyond my wildest dreams back then, everything you could possibly need or want in that big old town house down the long gravel driveway.

By the time we started going to the US, I had turned 11, but was so young that I just could not understand what was happening to me at times. When I tried to make a run for it to escape him on a street in Boston, he found me and took me back to the host family address.

In my mind's eye, I can still see the street where I ran from Roper's clutches. More recently, it has returned to me in my dreams. It was a line of residential houses, like you see in small town America. A TV series. A Hollywood movie.

As I race away from Roper, the mail boxes are there at the end of the neat, manicured gardens. Row upon row of those old-fashioned, wooden, colonial-style houses.

And I am running. Running, just to get away. Desperate to escape.

But I turn a corner and there is that grim figure, the *Umbro* tracksuit, the baggy pants. The spectre of my past. He has found me again. Warned me.

Never do that again. Do you understand?

Never. I repeat NEVER do that again.

Then he has taken me back.

When the kids from America came across to us on the exchange, Roper was so involved in our family life – for other reasons I will explain – that he used to stay over at the house and sleep in my room. A lad from the US team stayed with us.

Roper abused me during the night. The lad must have woken up or seen something and he asked if he could move out, to change the family he was staying with. It was agreed. He left;

still, there were no questions asked, no suspicions raised. Roper got away with it again.

The young lad, who was around 11 or 12 at the time, was obviously aware of what had gone on but probably did not fully understand. Still, he did not say anything. Even at that young age, I was thinking: *How much longer? How long will he get away with this?*

But it was not the kind of thing you mentioned to a friend or discussed in a dressing room before a game. Roper would have been there anyway most of the time – in the dressing room, giving me a lift back in his car, standing on the touchline during games. And it was not something I could open up about with my brothers when I got home.

On another trip, we went on tour to Ireland. My elder brother Anthony was around 15. He did not play in any of the Nova teams but came along for the holiday. He stayed with a family while I was playing. It was one of our first big adventures, and you cannot blame him for looking forward to a holiday with kids of his age.

We crossed on the ferry together from Liverpool, the kids running riot as they were so excited about going away. When we got to Ireland, Anthony went one way to stay with his family, and I went the other – with Roper. I realise now he had invited Anthony along with him as 'cover'. Neither of my brothers, none of my family had any way of knowing.

Anthony's Irish 'host' family got in touch with me after my story went public. It was so good of them, after all those years. And the message was one which I have heard many times since I decided to unlock the secrets of my past. *If only we had known, we would have helped you…we would have reported him.*

They apologised for everything – but it was nobody's fault except Roper's. And, of course, no one knew.

On the first trip to America, my brother Gary came because he was in the under-15 Nova team, a very good player in his own right. Gary would later go off to Wimbledon at 16 in a bid to start his own football career.

I know now that, once again, Roper had got him to come along as a front; I was only 11 years old, so he knew my parents would be worried, a kid of that age going away, and such a long way from home. Taking Gary was a way for him to reassure them. "His brother's there if he gets homesick," he would tell Mam and Dad.

Talking to my brothers now, I know that I said to my brother "Gary can I stay with you? Can I sleep in your bed?" Obviously, as he was three years older, he refused. He could not know the real reason for the question.

In any case, when we got to America, Roper made sure that he was with me and Gary stayed with a different family. That was Roper all over. The conniving, scheming paedophile who had worked every angle before we set off, made sure he had an answer to every question. He had been doing it for years to other families, long before he met me. It was a well-worn routine.

This happened to some of his victims 50 years ago; there will be those who have not told their loved ones, even after having kids and grandkids of their own. Some never will.

When I went public in 2016, I found a photo of me in a team shot by the plane in our silver team tracksuits, all with matching blue sports bags ready for the off. It had been buried in a box in my mother's home, along with a host of unwanted memories.

INNOCENCE LOST

I remember the excitement of Gary and all the other lads as we lined up; the excitement I could not share. But it was still the early days of the abuse.

You would not know it – how could you? – if you were my mother, my father, my auntie or uncle looking at that team photo. They would just be thinking: *there's our Paul, having a great time.*

But I can see the darkness in the eyes, the uneasy demeanour captured on that photo, with that poor excuse for a man right next to me; Roper, the proud coach, smiling for the camera, no doubt excited at what was to come, his best-laid plans working out all over again.

For the little boy beside him, there was nothing but utter dread; even now, there is no nostalgia looking back at that 'dream trip' to America.

Instead, the grainy '70s polaroid is a tiny window on a waking nightmare, a nightmare which had only just begun, but was to continue for years to come.

Chapter/5

MANHUNT

"Large vodka and soda and yes, I'm alright!"

I feel like I have to say something to some of my friends as I order a drink in the golf club.

"I'm still the same Stewy!"

People have treated me differently since I went public. They go out of their way to ask me if I'm okay. Lads I would have stood and had a chat with now feel inclined to say how brave I am. How hard it must have been. How they admire me for what I've done. It's not the same with my close mates. They still treat me as they always have done. But the less familiar acquaintances are different; it has changed.

It feels good that they are trying to support me; that they want to let me know they are behind me. It is heartwarming; I am grateful. But I am still me. I haven't changed. I'd come to terms with my life before my secret was out, so I don't want anything to change. I want to be normal.

It's a few months after I have gone public and I've headed to Portugal to play golf.

I'm meeting up with my old Spurs team-mate Steve Sedgley. It will be nice playing golf in the sun. We will go to Vilamoura, play on one of the courses where the fairways are tree-lined with the sun casting shadows on the smooth, perfectly kept greens. I take an early flight from Manchester to Faro. I meet up with Sedge in the hotel. It is the first time I have seen him since my story came out in the press.

"How are you, mate, you doing alright?"

I am asked the same things as I was by some of the lads back in Blackpool. We move on quickly and before too long, we talk about the usual stuff; helped by a few ice cold bottles of *Sagres*, the local brew. As often happens, the conversation drifts back to tales from our playing days.

The Gazza stories get another airing. The three pubs of Bahola. The frozen trout. The ostrich. The day he jumped over the fence for a ball which went missing in training – and we didn't see him again until the next day when he just turned up, shouting: 'I've found it!'

Sedge is still a good mate and the laughs are deep and genuine. Football is one of those careers where the strong bonds forged in the dressing room can remain for years. A flick through the contacts on my iPhone will reveal names from my playing days. I try to stay in touch; a players' union if you like.

We finish our drinks and head for bed, ready for the next day's game. It's a balmy Algarve night, tempered by a cool breeze. All is still and quiet. It's the first time I've been able to get away from it all. The laid-back vibe of Vilamoura seems a long way from the chilly autumn days of November last year.

•••••••

MANHUNT

When I went public in 2016, I could never have anticipated how big the reaction could be. How could I? It was a giant leap into the unknown for me. I was just an ex-footballer, now a regular businessman living in Blackpool doing a nine to five job, trying to get on with my life.

There were so many messages of support. I'm not great on social media but I know enough to find my way around. I've got just over 7,000 followers on Twitter last time I looked. It meant so much to have my old mates in football behind me.

'Wish my former Spurs team-mate, Paul Stewart all the very best. Extremely courageous in telling his story,' wrote Gary Lineker.

My old mate Bobby Mimms, the goalie at Tottenham, was one of the first to text me. Gareth Southgate, in one of his first interviews as England manager, paid tribute to my bravery in speaking out. We had played together for a short while at Crystal Palace, and it meant a great deal to me. While I had been expecting some negative comments, there was nothing but positive reaction and I was so grateful for that.

The BBC, ITV, Sky, and virtually every newspaper in the land were beating a path to my door. But it was the response from the other victims of childhood abuse – and my own family – which was so overwhelming.

Within hours of the paper hitting the streets, my old Manchester City team-mate David White revealed his own abuse for the first time.

It was another front page story and made headlines around the world, just as my story had done. It made me realise that our fame was a powerful tool in this fight to raise awareness of a taboo subject.

I dropped David a direct message on Twitter just to say 'I hope you're ok' and to assure him that we were all behind him. I knew from my own experience how much courage it took to go public.

A few days later, I spoke to him in person when we met up at the PFA offices. I was impressed how he handled himself during such a difficult time. Little did we realise all those years ago when we turned out in front of thousands every Saturday at Maine Road that we shared a common bond – though, of course, his situation was different to mine. David had already confided in his close family about the abuse. Just like me, he feared the consequences of his father taking justice into his own hands, so his dad went to the grave not knowing what happened to his son.

During that first week, Roper's victims came forward, one by one; the first within hours of my first interview appearing in the *Daily Mirror*; then a long line of others as the news spread.

Some came to me, some went straight to the police, while there were those who either contacted or were tracked down by various newspapers and TV stations. I made sure I replied to every victim who got directly in touch with me.

Through my new contacts in the press, I was aware there was a race to find Roper, an obvious desire for reporters, the police, even other victims, to bring him to justice. It became a race straight out of a crime novel as the cops got in touch with Interpol to check on his whereabouts.

I knew there were two newspapers going through dozens of potential addresses for 'Francis Roper'. Some confusion around his name hampered the enquiry because it turns out that his full name was 'James Francis Roper'.

It became apparent he had left the UK to live in Thailand more than 20 years earlier. Greater Manchester Police were looking for him there. Interpol confirmed they were helping with that inquiry.

Newspaper reporters and TV stations were asking me for my advice on his whereabouts. The last I had heard, there was a rumour about him being arrested on child sex offences in the Far East, dating back to the 1990s. My mam did recall hearing that, but we could find no historic reference to it in newspapers as it was the days before online editions. So we had to sit and wait to see if he could be found, by police – or journalists hot on his trail.

Meanwhile, the numbers rose over the weeks and months as the soccer abuse scandal grew. Police contacted me, and officers from Manchester came to do a video interview.

They set up the cameras in my house and we went through details of Roper's activity over a period of years, from 1975-79, when he abused me. It was all recorded as they looked not just at him but his potential links to other paedophiles operating in the game.

Another victim gave his account of how he had been abused by Roper, telling his family for the first time of his ordeal after reading my account. He was also interviewed by the police. He first got in touch at about 10am on the day my first interview appeared in the press and said that he knew 'straight away it was the same man, as soon as I read it.' He wanted me to know my story had given him the courage to tell his own family for the first time, and he thanked me.

"I came forward because of you," he told me. "I struggled with drink and drugs, to express love, even with my own children. I've told my mum who is elderly now. You gave me the courage to do that.

"I think *why didn't I stop him?* but it's hard when you are so young. I was away from home at a tournament. I was only 13, I was so vulnerable."

You can imagine how I felt hearing it – a story so similar to my own. Years later, that same victim recalled seeing Roper with a group of young lads on the touchline as he played in a senior game.

"I thought I *bet he will try it all over again with them*," he said. It made him sick to think the cycle of abuse had gone on long after he left Nova. He called for Roper to be brought to justice.

Ex-Crewe and Sheffield Utd player Andy Woodward, who also waived his right to anonymity after falling victim to another coach, also spoke out in support of me. "There were tears when I read it, I was really moved by his account and I have only got heartfelt praise in the way that he is trying to help others.

"This has caused so much destruction and upset in the personal lives of the victims.

"When Paul spoke about his suicidal thoughts, it made me think of the many young players who never made it as professionals and are no longer with us. One victim took his life at 30. There will be so many others."

Of course, I wanted Roper caught. So did Bev and the kids. But we also knew that it was going to be hard to track him down. If he were still alive, he could be in his 70s or 80s.

Another former pro came forward to say he had preyed on him when he was 12. Those attacks came 13 years after I was first abused, confirming Roper had got away with his vile exploitation with generations of kids, before and after me.

Roper was so keen to groom that lad that he took him to watch me when I was playing for Manchester City in the 1987/88 season. By then, he was not only going to City – and bragging about how he had coached me as a kid – his grooming involved trips to Manchester United's training ground, The Cliff, again buying them gifts, giving cash, and sports gear.

Failing that, there were days out on the amusements in Blackpool. After I left, he got the nickname 'Roper the Groper'. Apparently it became the 'team joke' by the late 1980s, when his reputation was well known among those working alongside him in the leagues of Manchester junior football.

One former pro, now 41, said: "I realise now that he must have been doing it for years and years. He would spoil me rotten, it was all part of the grooming process. He took me to see Paul Stewart when he was playing for Manchester City.

"He would also take me for meals, tell me about his time working with Paul – it was 'Paul this and Paul that.' When Paul came out with his story, I thought *that must be him*.

"He experienced what I experienced. It is hard to believe he still took me to see him after all he had done to Paul. There must be so many others."

Roper invited him to sleep in his bed when he was homesick, playing a game away from home. He had not spoken about it before, even to his own family. He described being abused while staying at a Blackpool B&B: "I was homesick and vulnerable and he said to come down to his bedroom. He assaulted me, he knew I was very young and missing my family.

"He would not leave it so I said I would sleep in the bed with him. Even at that age I was thinking *this is unusual*. I was very reluctant, but he convinced me.

"He put his hands on me and I jumped up and ran along the corridor to see the guy who ran the B&B. Roper was panicking and shouting 'don't worry, don't worry, he is homesick.'

"After that he tried to buy my silence. He opened a drawer full of gold rings and jewellery and said 'take what you want.' He would give me sports gear, bags of it, £10 to play on the amusements, which was a lot of money in those days.

"I had buried those memories for so many years, but they would still come to the surface. Every time I saw abuse on TV, on the news, or an item about the Savile inquiry, it came into my mind again. It would stay there for days.

"It affected me way back then because I could not hug my mum, I became very cold and my parents noticed. I have never told them, right to this day. That is the message. You have to talk about it."

He was a player with a lower league club. As he came forward, he was joined by some of the biggest names in football as the abuse investigation moved right across the UK.

Wayne Rooney, captain of England, urged all those who had been affected to come forward.

Alan Shearer did the same in his role as patron of the NSPCC. It became public that a Southampton coach, involved in the youth team set-up when Shearer was there as a teenager, was under investigation.

Matt Le Tissier gave an interview to the BBC in which he spoke about certain massage techniques and how he thought they were inappropriate during his time as a young player at the club where he spent his entire career.

•••••••••

Crimewatch did a tremendous job in further highlighting the issue. Hundreds of potential victims came forward after one of the most successful appeals in the history of the show, which first went out in 1984.

The police unit investigating child abuse in football received more than 400 new referrals. About 23 per cent relate to the sport at professional level, some dating back to the 1970s, but with others as recent as 2016. Victims were as young as four years old.

Figures showed the national abuse investigation, codenamed Operation Hydrant, had received 1,432 referrals by the end of March. Around a third of the latest allegations centred on the North West. I knew that could mean even more victims of Roper.

As time went on, it was still unclear if Roper was alive.

While living in Thailand, he had apparently been working for his chain of sports shops, buying and sourcing materials and also taking his youth teams there en route to tournaments Down Under. There were potential leads on an address once used by his elderly mother, and a search for siblings who might still be alive.

It became public knowledge that he had started with Nova in the mid-'70s and gone on abusing boys in the '80s and '90s, working with Blackpool during Sam Ellis's tenure at the club, up to 1989, and beyond.

There is no suggestion anyone in authority had any idea what Roper was up to. I could never bring myself to tell my Blackpool coaches or even Sam what I had suffered as a youngster. That is one of the things I regret most…the feeling that I could have prevented others suffering.

But the club trusted Roper, who regularly attended games and ferried schoolboys to matches. It would take a lot for a teenage boy to question someone who was given such authority and who held a position of such stature within the club.

Any lad trying to make his way in the game wouldn't want to rock the boat at the football club that had given them their chance, let alone blow the whistle on a paedophile. How would it look? The word of a teenager against the word of an established scout and well respected junior coach?

Looking back now, I can see that it would have been difficult; even if I had somehow managed to find a way to tell people. Times are different now, though some of the same obstacles remain.

The victims coming forward had sparked a worldwide search for Roper. Their accounts all told the same story. The treats. The trips to the beach. The gifts of kit, the visits to his shop. Then, of course, he would start the abuse.

Many spoke of the four-storey Stockport home where he lived alone, and tormented me and countless other victims. It made me sick to think he took kids who he was grooming to see me play, bragging about how he had coached me in the early days. I am glad that I did not know about that in a way; it would have brought back all those memories of the abuse.

I wondered for years how he got away with it.

The answer was – as it was with so many other abusers, including Jimmy Savile – the fear of the victims themselves.

Bev, many parents and the kids were of the view that he should be brought before the courts, made to pay for what he had done. Of course that was a view shared by my brothers – though they were naturally worried about the trauma of such a court case, not just for me, but for Mam and Dad – and almost all the other victims.

For me, there was also the knowledge of the victims who had not come forward, who could not face the ordeal of going through the police interviews, telling their loved ones.

For those whose secrets were still locked away, there was no question of me giving them away. I made the decision not to say anything about anyone who had confided in me. Many had elected to keep it from their family and loved ones.

Though they may have given up clues as to what happened to Roper – even where he was now – there was no real justification in my view for asking them to get involved. Especially after all this time.

My decision to go public had come after 41 long years, but it was mine alone. I knew all about that silence; locking away the past. You cannot say they are wrong to make that choice; it is different for everyone.

Chapter/6

THE SOUND OF SILENCE

It's 1974. A typical rainy day in Manchester. Sunday means one thing. Game day. Nova are in the Under-11s division and today is a big game against our local rivals. We play on the local pitches, they're not the best, bumpy and uneven and today we will finish caked in mud from head to toe but we don't care. When we score a goal and glance over to see the smiles on our parents' faces, this could be Old Trafford or even Wembley.

Today we're in yellow and White Hill will wear blue and white. They have some good players. Our team isn't too bad either, made up of lads from the county teams. It's always between us and them who wins the league and the cups. If we're not playing White Hill we win 10, 12, even 15-0. Walkovers with no winners; scoring practice for us and demoralising for the other teams and the poor keepers who have to keep picking the ball out of the net.

The parents are lined up on opposite sides of the pitch as the game starts. It often feels to us lads in the team that they want this as much as we do. We can hear their shouts and screams; cheers when we score and frustration when we misplace a pass. As always, my mam Joyce and dad Bert are there, loyal to the last, watching every game I played in, no matter the weather. If my older brother Gary was playing on the same day, Dad would go and see him. Mam would follow my team; if not, they would both come along, my mother an ever-present, season after season. 'Go on Paul', she would cry as I played.

If the parents got excited, then the coaches could be worse.

The White Hill coach means business and looks the part in his tracksuit. He is standing next to my mam on the touchline. There is a little black lad who is in his team, playing on the wing. The coach is on his case. 'Take him on!' 'Beat your man' 'Get your crosses in!' he shouts, that kind of thing. Then, as the game goes on, it gets more intense. A few swear words are thrown in.

Maybe the coach just wants to win the game and he thinks he's trying to get the best out of his player but it doesn't sound like that to my mam who sees the lad's head go down every time he shouts from the touchline. Soon, she can take no more and decides she needs to stick up for the lad.

"Leave him alone, how do you expect him to play when you are shouting at him like that?" she tells him.

"Shut up you old bag!" comes back the instant response. The coach obviously hadn't realised my mam wasn't on her own.

Without a second's thought, my dad goes over to him, grabs his tracksuit by the scruff of the neck with his big hands and nuts him.

The coach goes flying. There's a melee as other people get

involved, trying to break it up. I see my mam lose her footing in the chaos and she gets mud on her new coat. My dad stands over the coach. He waits for him to get up – standing, ready, in case he thinks about fighting back. There's no chance of that.

Other coaches – including Roper – come running to the scene. Things start to settle down but there's no way the game can continue; the match is abandoned.

The players of both teams start to file away, walking off the pitch; some talking with their mates, some going over to their parents. As I'm walking away I glance back and see Roper. He's writing the little winger's name on his hand in biro. The lad's a good player. Roper wasn't one to allow a touchline bust-up to get in the way of business.

Mam and Dad get back to the car and the coach is there.

"Come on then!" says Dad, who is ready, in case he wants to get his own back. But the coach knows he faces another hiding if my dad gets hold of him, so there is no more fighting.

••••••••

I knew exactly what my dad had done to that coach during that game and it did not surprise me in the least. Dad was always a tough nut; his children and immediate family all knew that, from a very early age.

If my dad had known back then what he knows now, Roper would not have survived. And Dad would have had to be held accountable for his actions, no matter how justified. He would have been taken from us, put behind bars.

That episode, the fight on the touchline, and my dad's way of protecting his family, played on my mind as I contemplated going public and speaking about my childhood abuse, waiving my right to anonymity, for the first time in 41 years.

What I had learned during all the time I had kept my secret – almost all my adult life – I had learned the hard way: that the abuse impacts not just on you, but everyone around you, and I needed them to understand how and why I was coming forward.

I know my mam has gone through a horrific ordeal with the very thought of what Roper did to her son. She wakes in the morning thinking about it, and is kept awake by the thought of how he got away with it. But she could not have known, because I was too scared to tell her. It has taken four decades to find the courage to speak out for the first time.

Mam is 77 now, and Dad 79. I broke the news to Bev and my close family in the restaurant in Manchester on the same day I first read that story in *The Mirror*. After arriving home the next day, I knew it was important to speak to my parents next.

Mam and Dad live in a static caravan park on the outskirts of the town. Quite a few retired people live there. They moved up to Blackpool to be closer to the family some years ago.

I rang Mam first to let her know I was coming. They would often go to a local car boot sale on Sunday mornings and it was unusual for me to be visiting at that time, especially without Bev or the kids. Mam sensed straight away that something wasn't right.

"What's up?" she asked. It crossed my mind that she might have thought I had started drinking heavily again or something like that was going on.

"It's nothing," I reassured her. "I'll be over in two minutes."

As I knocked on the door, they were pleased to see me. Little did they know I was about to have the kind of conversation with them I had never had before. They could not know as they greeted me with warm smiles that over the course of the next week, my face would be plastered on the front pages of newspapers and on TV screens.

After the niceties of making some tea and coffee, I sat down to tell them what I was going to do.

Just like the time I told Bev and my brother and sister-in-law in San Carlo, I didn't know where to start. But I found the words in the end.

And when I told them, it was overwhelming.

There was a short, silent pause as they both stopped to take in the enormity of what I was getting off my chest. It wasn't long before they gave me their unconditional support.

They told me how proud they were of me and assured me that I was doing the right thing. Mam especially understood that this was something I had to do; that it would help me come to terms with what had happened all those years ago.

They might have suspected that some physical abuse had taken place but never sexual. That was a complete shock. As I knew he would, Dad said simply that he would have killed Roper if he would have known.

"You couldn't possibly have known," I told them. "I want you to understand that at no stage have you ever done anything to let me down."

They had simply been loving parents who had been hood-winked by an evil paedophile using every trick in the book to pull the wool over their eyes.

I told them that I couldn't do what I was doing without their blessing.

"If you don't want me to speak out, then I won't do. If it's going to make you feel uncomfortable then I'll say nothing."

Mam and Dad assured me I was doing the right thing. Just as they always have been, they were on my side. "If it helps you, son, we're right behind you."

••••••••

When he moved in on me, Roper knew that he had to groom my family as well as me. He knew how things worked.

As soon as I joined his team, he made sure he was a regular visitor to Cleeve Road. At any given opportunity, he'd look to strike up a cheery conversation with Mam and Dad. *Your Paul played well today, scored loads of goals.* He'd tell them I was the best thing since sliced bread and that I was going places. Mam and Dad must have liked him. He appeared like a normal bloke who was good company. He was well mannered, always had something to say and couldn't be more helpful when it came to me and my football.

Roper especially targeted my mam. Every time he saw her, he would always make a point of giving her some kit for me or my brothers. There would be boots, trainers, tracksuits, tops. Mam would also get sports gear and household appliances – TV, a stereo – material things which he knew we could not afford.

Before I knew Roper, I would wear boots which were hand-me-downs from my brothers. Then he would turn up on the doorstep with a carrier bag and pull out an expensive-looking branded box. He would open it up, pull the tissue paper back and there would be a shiny new pair of *adidas* boots. Of course, my parents were impressed. They just thought he was doing it because he wanted to help me with my football. Roper would lap it up. *Imagine the goals you'll score in them, Paul.* I was soon walking around in all the latest gear.

The gifts started coming thick and fast. Once, I remember he got me the latest Atari video game for the telly. I had it long before other kids in school. It was the kind of gift that earned Roper instant kudos.

He got away with it because he was so 'trusted', and never gave my parents, my brothers, even my grandparents any reason to suspect anything untoward. My parents thought he was a great lad and would never think twice about what he was up to, why he was with me all the time. These days it might arouse suspicion but you have to remember they were very different times in the 1970s.

As time developed, Roper was so confident in his position of trust, he would stay over before matches at the weekend. He would stay at the house in order to be able to get into my bedroom. He did not always stay over. Sometimes he left at 11pm. But that was because he had already done what he wanted to do.

When he did stay at the house, it was natural that he would then say 'I will drop him off at school' or he would take us all to the game because we did not have a car. At the time, it was so easy for him to dupe us.

The next day, he would take the 'team' out for treats, like going to the cinema to see the latest *Star Wars* or *Superman* film, like he was some shining light. But I knew it was just to get me alone. My brother Anthony thought until recently that Roper had been taking the entire team training when he came to take me away. They all ask now: 'Why? How?'

But then, he gave them no reason to suspect.

Mam, in fact, started to fall for his charms because he was giving her everything she did not have in a material way. It was not like he was chatting her up; I am not convinced he had any sexual interest in women, only young boys. But she was bound to be impressed by Roper. He always seemed to have cash; he was a successful businessman. She thought he was going to be the key to my future, my career as a footballer, and the same was true for Gary, before he headed off to Wimbledon to try and make it in the game. It was all part of how he got in with the family to get to me.

Going to the bowling alley and restaurants were things we never did because we could not afford to. The gifts, the days out, the trips abroad were all a way of ingratiating himself.

You can see how it would all work. Just picture the scene. It's a Saturday night and as me and my brothers are playing footy outside on a summer's evening, the Fiat pulls up outside the house. My heart sinks. There's Roper with two takeaway bags that smell divine. The door opens. *Bite to eat? I've got some Chinese here...plenty to go round...*

Before long he's got his feet under the table enjoying a Saturday night treat with my family.

Freebies and trips to America? Why wouldn't it look good? It was all part of Roper's evil plan.

After the takeaway was finished, he'd make himself comfortable on the sofa watching telly like a favourite uncle over for a visit. Then it was payback time.

"Game tomorrow, Paul. And then we could do with some extra training. You know what you've got to do if you want to be a footballer..."

THE SOUND OF SILENCE

Innocent enough small talk to Mam and Dad and my brothers but every word sent a shiver down my spine.

••••••••

I was 'struck dumb' in those early years with Roper. I remember Mam telling my wife-to-be, Bev, that I did not speak for a year. Obviously Mam did not know then why that was.

At the time, I remember that my Aunt Jean was concerned.

"What is to do with our Paul? He never opens his mouth now, and he was such a happy lad," she asked my mam. "He was never like that, there is something wrong somewhere."

They had seen me growing up, when I went to their house – just a short hop from ours – and played with their children. They remembered the carefree lad with the mop of curly hair, always laughing and joking. I had always been an outgoing kid; I made records and sang for my mam, I loved to be playing with other kids outdoors.

As I moved through my early teenage years, they could see a massive change in me that couldn't be explained simply by the onset of adolescence alone. Roper's influence was growing with every passing day and it seemed the easiest and safest thing to do; to retreat in to a world of my own.

Roper was manipulating me and driving me against my family but my family wouldn't let me avoid him because they thought he was helping me to fulfil my football dream. And I couldn't say anything about the abuse because I was scared; I thought the lives of my mam and dad and brothers were in danger. If I was silent, perhaps all the problems would just go away.

My family recall me being unable to start a conversation,

though naturally I still went to school, and would always speak when spoken to. But there was a conscious withdrawal, a deep-seated character change which worried them.

Roper was always in our house and I knew that whenever he heard me talk, he was judging me. If I said the wrong thing, there might be a back-hander later that night. *Why did you say that? I've told you not to talk about that!* In my mind, it became easier not to talk at all.

I would not strike up conversation with anyone, even at school. Mam put it down to teenage years kicking in; to football; to the pressures of trying to make it in the game I loved. She feels a terrible guilt now I have finally come forward.

We realise now it was a cry for help, a tell-tale sign of a kid unable to understand what was happening to him, and hoping someone would take care of the situation.

I'm no psychologist, but I think that I wanted someone to say 'Paul, what's going on?' It never happened because Roper was so careful. He managed situations between me and my family and made sure the opportunity never arose for them to think anything untoward was going on.

At school, the change in my character made me unpopular. No surprise when I didn't speak to anyone. At primary school, I had friends like any normal kid would have. It all changed in secondary school. I don't know if I appeared angry, big-headed or arrogant to the other kids, but I would often end up just kicking the ball against the wall alone if I was not involved in a game in the yard. Roper did not want me to have friends. It was partly control again, maybe in case I said something.

Those feelings of anger and isolation stayed with me later in life and it is a pattern seen with many victims like me.

THE SOUND OF SILENCE

My mother was working as an auxiliary nurse at the local hospital by the time I reached 14, and she would ring the house early in the morning to make sure I was up when everyone had gone out.

"Are you up Paul? Get yourself off to school. Make sure you have something to eat," she would tell me.

I often went straight back to bed, and then went into school to play football, then onto my nana Ethel Edgerton's house. I spent a lot of time there with my mum working full time. The school was just a stone's throw from my nana's house, where she lived with husband Sid.

I always remember that she had a painting on the wall of a boy with a tear running down his face, these were seen a lot in houses years ago, it was either a boy or girl, looking really sad and I used to think the artist must have been thinking of me when he painted it. Those paintings were said by some to be cursed. There was a poem alongside it which read:

Happiness is like a butterfly,
always just beyond your reach,
but if you sit down quietly,
it will alight upon you

I always wanted to be in that poem, but always felt like the boy. I was growing up now. I'd been under Roper's spell for what felt like a long time. The one light at the end of the tunnel had been following my dream to be a footballer. That had been my lifeline.

Without that, I don't know if I would have survived.

Chapter/7

REBEL WITH A CAUSE

Despite the turmoil in my young life, I was blossoming as a footballer.

Right from the age of 11 or 12, I attracted the attention of club scouts. At times there were several clubs chasing my signature, so they must have liked what they saw. Scouts would approach my parents on the touchline and ask if I fancied going to their club for a couple of weeks, often during the school summer holidays. I remember loads of letters dropping on the doormat asking me to go for a trial.

I went to the two big clubs on my doorstep: Manchester United and Manchester City. But for whatever reason, even when I was young, I still felt that I would have a better chance of making it at a lower division club. So I went to places like Coventry and Bury too. I didn't like Coventry, being so far from home didn't feel right.

Wherever I went, Roper would be with me, watching my every

move. He was a scout for Blackpool, so it was obviously in his interest to point me in that direction. He controlled everything. Roper had convinced me and my family that it was in my best interests. *You'll get in the team, get plenty of experience, then the big clubs might come in for you. That's the way to go, Paul.*

As it happens, Blackpool really liked me. The former Northern Irish football hero Peter Doherty was involved in the set-up. I should have signed schoolboy forms when I was 14 but they took me on a year early. He kept the forms in his top drawer ready for when I was old enough. He also assured me of an apprenticeship at 16 and that I would only have to serve a year after that before I turned professional.

Throughout the early years, Roper would take me up to Blackpool. For training sessions and then longer visits during the summer holidays, he would pick me up in Manchester and then the two of us would be in his car for the hour or a bit more that it took to get there. I'd be in the front seat while his powerful stereo blasted out Jerry Lee Lewis tunes. *Chantilly Lace. Johnny B Goode.* All the hits would be played. He'd got me exactly where he wanted me.

After training, we would go out and about, enjoying all that Blackpool had to offer to young kids like me. We'd go on the amusements along the seafront; Roper giving us plenty of change for the fruit machines and arcade games. Or we'd go to the *Pleasure Beach* on some of the rides. Cash was no problem to Roper; he'd throw money around like confetti. As you can imagine, Blackpool was a big thrill to a normal kid from a council estate like me.

On the pitch, I think I was developing into a strong character. I think that what was happening to me with Roper made me even more determined to succeed. It ignited a spark of burning ambition in me. I'd do anything to make it. Football gave me a reason to be able to cope with what I was going through. It also gave me an opportunity to express myself – something that was becoming harder and harder in everyday life. It was a simple game that came naturally to me. Within the confines of those white lines, I was safe and free to be myself.

I made my mind up quite early on that I was not going to be left on the bench or forgotten about by the coaches. I would force them to notice me. I'd had a disappointing experience when I first started playing for Manchester Boys. It came when I made a guest appearance on *Jim'll Fix It*. Given my ordeal with Roper, the irony of appearing in that programme isn't lost on me. You couldn't make it up.

It came about when our Manchester Boys captain wrote to the now notorious paedophile Jimmy Savile and asked him if he could 'fix it' for us to play Manchester United at under-11. Jim did indeed fix it for us.

It was a dream come true to be playing United and at Old Trafford, too. Even the great Bobby Charlton made a guest appearance, playing for us against the United team of 1975. It was a 3-3 draw but I never got a run-out and spent the entire match on the substitutes' bench.

The lad next to me could not stop crying because he never got a game. He just sat there and wept. I was gutted at not getting a chance to play against some of my all-time heroes. I never forgot that, and became even more determined never to miss out on an experience like this again.

The Manchester Boys captain went to meet Jimmy on our behalf. His letter was read out and shown on screen. We all got badges – I didn't keep mine, it was a tiny, plastic thing and not like the shiny, silver pendant with a red ribbon that you saw on the TV. I remember the disappointment when I got it, thinking: *Is this it?*

When Savile was arrested I told my friends that I went on *Jim'll Fix It* and they told me, half in jest, that I was a 'near miss'. They were completely unaware of my past at the time. I said nothing, probably just smirked and agreed with them. There are so many connections with Roper, even in the latest investigation undertaken by the police into the historical football abuse scandal.

·········

There was no pattern to the nature of the abuse that I suffered over the course of the four years. It was all down to Roper. It was a case of whatever came into his head that he wanted to do to me. It nearly always started with him in the driving seat and his hand drifting over towards me in the passenger seat. Roper was precise and careful, though he did get more complacent as time went on.

There were some near misses along the way, times when he came so close to being caught. He risked so much to get away with what he was doing, driven by his dark desires, and it happened so often that there was bound to be the odd time when he aroused suspicion.

On one occasion, when I was 13 or 14, my parents came into the house and they found me sitting on the settee sobbing. It might have been a Sunday morning and I might have returned home after my game while Mam and Dad were still out watching

Gary. Roper, of course, had let himself in with me when he had dropped me off.

"What the bloody hell's going on?" asked Mam or Dad.

Quick as a flash, Roper was on the scene and replied: "He's crying because he thinks Gary is going to make it as a footballer, and he might not now."

Nothing could have been further from the truth, of course, but it must have sounded plausible to my parents. They knew how important my football dream was, so why wouldn't I have been upset for a reason like that? He had sweet-talked his way out of it again.

Another time, Mam was packing shirts for Roper to sell and raise funds for yet another Nova tour. While she was there, she met another parent who told her he had seen Roper thumping one of his young players in the leg after training.

I know now that it was a lad who he also abused, the same victim I would meet in a pub years later. Roper claimed it was because he had done something wrong in footy practice. He had him up against the car. My mother was blazing with anger when she heard that, asking the dad: "Why did you not stop him?" But he said that he just thought it was something to do with tactics, a petty row over training. All these episodes were clues to what was really going on.

I remember I would get horrendous stomach pains as I sat in the back of Roper's car. I thought at the time it was because I was nervous about the upcoming game, but I realise now it was due to the fear of what I was going to have to endure later. I had to lie flat sometimes, I was in so much agony.

Then, when I was around 13, I had shingles, and was in severe pain for a week, forced to sleep on the settee at home. It was a classic sign of stress, the result of my body reacting to the extreme pressure my mind was under. Roper always came to call when I was sick.

Then, when I was about 14, I ended up in plaster just as I was getting into the youth team set-up. I had developed tenosynovitis; a physical problem that affected my ankles and in turn, my achilles tendon. It was all to do with the way my body was changing as I grew up.

I was in the house, putting my legs up, when my mother came home from work. There was Roper, alone with me again in the house. He had no reason to be there because I clearly couldn't play football but he would make up some excuse about why he was there. *I'm just keeping an eye on the patient. Won't be long before he's out of that plaster and scoring goals again!*

He even turned up once on Christmas Day when we were on the way to our grandmother's house with all the presents.

My mam could see that I was lagging behind before she spotted his car. She was quite rightly furious, and said to me: "Is he mithering you for football training again?" She put her foot down on that occasion, and off to Nana's we did go as Roper's car headed in the opposite direction.

Mam was always looking out for me and on one occasion tried to cut all ties with Roper after she knew he had stepped over the line.

I came running in after football and my mother knew that Roper had hit me. He turned up at the house later to try and explain and she punched him squarely on the jaw.

"Don't ever darken my door again!" she told him in no uncertain terms. You could hear the smack on his face from upstairs.

But he managed somehow to get back in with my family. There was the football; I wanted to be in the team, and so would beg my parents to let me play again. And Roper always came back. That was the thing that haunts me most, even now. He would never give in.

•••••••

When I was 14, my older brother Gary got an apprenticeship at Wimbledon under Dario Gradi – before his days at Crewe – and it meant I was often at home alone.

I had a 90 per cent absence rate in my final year. School held no interest for me as I had already signed forms at Blackpool. Making it in football was all that interested me. I was convinced I was going to make it, so I had a 'couldn't care less' attitude about school.

I remember doing algebra in maths one day and as I sat at the back staring out of the class window, my maths teacher shouted out at me: "What are you up to Stewart?"

I leaned back on my chair and responded by saying: "I would never go to my local shop and ask for $a + b = y$."

As often would happen, I was sent to the headmaster's office. Every time I was there I was told: "You do know, Paul, very few make it as professional footballers."

My reply was always the same. "I WILL make it." It was what I told all the teachers when they gave me a lecture about my future. They always told me to study, in case it did not work out.

I actually tried to go to Blackpool a year early, which caused the club serious problems. I was so desperate to get my football career up and running that I lied about my age. I was 15 but said I was 16, which was old enough to start an apprenticeship. I actually left home and started training with them but then the school board came into the club.

Questions were asked and I was soon sent back to Mam and Dad's. Blackpool were fined £15,000 and I had to go back to school. It made no difference; I simply waited until I was old enough to leave, and went to Blackpool a year later. They told me I had to do my exams but I just walked into the exam hall and then walked straight out and back to the house. Nothing mattered to me except football. I wish now I had listened to them as I had to re-educate myself in later life. I left without a single qualification.

••••••••

As I returned to my childhood home recently, another vivid memory from my teenage years came flooding back.

I am 15, much bigger physically by now, and Roper is moving forward in that car again, on the road leading to my home.

We are not far away from our house on Cleeve Road and he is about to drop me off after a game or training session. There is some sort of argument or he is moaning at me as he often would. *What were you doing there? You can play better than that. You've let yourself down. You're not doing as I've told you.* That sort of thing.

Then he leans toward me as is the usual routine. His hand moves towards my groin; I know instinctively what he wants. I have lived through this scenario hundreds of times before. Except, this time, I have had enough.

The car is still moving but I push him away with all my might and open the car door. He slams his foot on the brake and the car screeches to a halt.

I know he will be blazing with anger at such a show of insolence, so I jump out of the car and run as fast as I can to get home; so fast he cannot catch me. I feel my trainers pounding on the concrete of the pavements and the road as I dodge cars and duck and weave around trees and people along the roads leading to the safety of our front door. I'm quick and fit, so it doesn't take long.

I arrive on our doorstep, barely out of breath, but agitated. I look around. There is no sign of his car. Mam and Dad let me into the house and ask me why I'm crying. "What's the matter? Has he been hitting you?" they ask. I don't say anything. I'm just hoping and praying that I will not hear the sound of the knocker and see him in the doorway. There could be some beating if he finds me; I will be black and blue. But I hear nothing. He does not come to our door.

•••••••••

That was the last time I was with him.

It was over.

Four long years of abuse had come to an end. Countless encounters in his Fiat saloon were now just a dark and bitter secret. A secret I would never fully reveal until much, much later in life.

Until I was a middle-aged man.

I hadn't planned to lash out at him that day; it just happened. I had finally snapped. I could take no more.

I will never know what he thought back then.

Perhaps he had already started to move on to his next, younger victim. Whether he feared I was going to tell my parents at long last, I don't know. I never asked, because I never had to deal with him again.

There were no questions from Mam and Dad why Roper had disappeared from our lives. They knew that I was heading off to Blackpool soon anyway.

I had finally escaped. Now I could try and start living the rest of my life.

Chapter/8

MAM AND DAD'S STORY

Every parent's worst nightmare

Mam's Story

I am Joyce Stewart.

I met my husband Bert in Wythenshawe when I was 14. He had moved in down the street; one of my friends said there was 'a good looking lad just got that house down there.'

We have been married for 58 years now. His family first came to the area when Bert was 16. I used to have to pass his house to get to Sale Circle shops. I went to the shops all the time for my mother and it meant I could meet him. I was in a gang of girls and we used to look out for him. I have to say that because it is true – he is a bighead anyway!

One day he brought a purse out, threw it up in the air and I caught it. I left school at 15 but I used to wait for Bert to come down the road from his job at the flower shop. I got collared once by my dad for doing that, he was watching me from our toilet window and saw me standing around and said: "What are you waiting around for lads for?"

Bert and I had many fall-outs over those teenage years. When we did, he used to take my friends out to make me jealous. We always got back together and would start courting again.

I had three sisters and a brother; he had four brothers and two sisters, so there was not much room at home. There is my eldest sister Jean, 83, Mildred, 80, Anne, 74, David, 68. Growing up, my mam would leave porridge for us in the stove and Dad would take us to school if he was not on an early shift. They both worked really hard, and we followed their example.

Mildred worked with me in the delicatessen we owned when Paul first signed for Manchester City; but we had jobs in a market in Blackpool before that, selling towels and tea towels, making soft toys for the church to sell. We did anything to provide for the kids, to save up to open our own business.

We would stay at Mrs T's, the B&B where Paul later stayed in Blackpool as a young player. We were there through the week, then we would go home at the weekends. We did that for a few months to get the money together to start the deli. I got my first job in *Littlewoods*, then later, when the kids were older, as a care worker in hospital. I worked all my life.

I first moved to Wythenshawe with my parents, Ethel, a mill worker, and Sydney, who had a job at the gas works.

It was fantastic. Our house had three bedrooms, a parlour and a garden – my mam loved the garden, and I think I have got that from her.

Before we moved there, we had been in a little 'two up and two down' in Manchester. I slept in one bed with my sisters and

oking back:
vealing my
ildhood secret
the world has
en difficult –
nought I'd take
o the grave

Paulee Doo: I was a curly-haired kid full of smiles and mischief before Frank Roper came on to the scene. Above left: 28 Cleeve Road – where I kicked my first ball and dreamed of making it

Happy family: With Dad, Mam, Gary (second from right), Anthony (far right) and dog Mimi!

Face of evil: Frank Roper looks like just another football coach on the team photo – no one knew what he was really like

Dream trip: Lining up with Nova team-mates ready to board the plane for the United States. An exciting time for many but, for me, a recurring nightmare. Right: On one of the US trips, wearing a cap that George Best signed

Home from home: (Left) Host family Ed and Doreen pictured with me on a trip to the US. They took a real shine to me – so Roper got me moved. Right: Getting noticed –picking up an award

A different life: In a Chinese restaurant during one of the summer trips and (right) staying with another family in America

If only we had known: Me (in the West Ham shirt) and Anthony (right) during our trip to Ireland. We stayed with a wonderful family who suspected something wasn't quite right between me and Roper

Turning pro: In action for Blackpool during the 1980s and (left) a signed picture, which proudly hangs in The Old Town Hall in Poulton

Maine man: Signing for my home town club Manchester City with Jimmy Frizzell. (Right) I was asked to pull on a City shirt before a deal had been agreed!

KEEP UP THE GOOD WORK ... YOU'LL DO FOR ME & MOST CITY FANS .... REGARDS

PS - WROTE THIS BEFORE YESTERDAYS PERFORMANCE - TREMENDOUS BY ALL THE LADS & PRATIC YOURSELF KK

Heading to the top: Going for a flying header. My goals at City started to get me noticed by the top clubs and made me popular with the supporters

Happy couple: I did everything to make sure that Bev enjoyed her special day

All together now:
I went on to have one
of my best seasons
after Adam was born.
My career was taking
off – but I would
soon be separated
from my family

Double deal: Signing in at Tottenham with boss Terry Venables. Living with Gazza would be an adventure to say the least!

White heat: I had to wait for my chance to pull on a Spurs shirt. The goals didn't come easy and I soon started to feel the pressure

Haunting memories: Looking back over the playing fields where Roper used to take me and (top) back on Cleeve Road. I can't allow him to impact on my life now

my parents were in the other room, with an outside toilet. We could not believe the space we had when we got to our new place. It was so much better for us.

It was tougher for Bert because he had four brothers and two sisters, and one of the sisters married and moved in as well, so it was a great deal harder for him.

I was 19 when we married, and Bert was 21. We were really close as a family. Paul, Gary and Anthony were really good kids but Bert was very strict with them. They had to be in by seven every night – even in the summer – and when they came in, his first words were 'right, wash and bed.' They did grumble a bit sometimes because some nights their mates would keep coming to the door but he never let them out again. We went everywhere with the boys in those days.

Gary and Paul were always playing out together; Gary thought Paul was his because he was born on his third birthday. They were thick as thieves playing football. They used to rib Antony all the time; but he kept an eye on them as he was that bit older. They were happy kids and got on well together; Paul had so many curls when he was born we used to say he looked like a little girl, to be honest – he was a lovely kid, always happy and full of energy.

Paul used to tell me absolutely everything, no matter what it was, until Frank Roper came on the scene. His silence, when he barely spoke a word for such a long time, we put down to his desperate desire to be a footballer. It is only now that I realise that we were groomed by Roper too.

When Roper first approached us, I didn't really think twice about letting Paul play, but why would you? He seemed like he was trying to help him become a footballer, which is what he wanted more than anything in the world at that age. I was so taken in.

He groomed us, did everything he could to get in with the family. Back then, in the '70s, you never read or heard about abuse; it was never out in the open in the way that it is now, on TV, in the papers. If Paul's dad had found out what Roper was doing, he would have murdered him.

Roper told us once he had been engaged but it never worked out so he never bothered again. He also told us that he lived with his mother and sister in Stockport. I do not believe any of that now. But it was not the sort of thing you would go and check out.

When I think of it now, it makes me feel sick, that I trusted him to that extent. Roper would give Paul so much gear; tracksuits, trainers and so on, and he bought me ladies' sports kit. He was paying me, bribing me to get to Paul, but I did not realise, and had no way of knowing.

Roper even left shirts for us to sell to make him money. We used to go to his house sometimes for meetings, all the mums from the Nova team, and that was how he got the money together to take the team on the trips abroad. Roper took Paul and Anthony to Ireland, and they went on tour to America three times.

We went to warehouses with him to get the gear, and then he sold it off at a profit in his shops. It sickens me now to think what he was really about. Not only was he using us to get to Paul, he even had us selling his kit for him. He was utterly shameless.

We even visited him at his house in Stockport to sort it all out. I know now that he took Paul there. It is terrible to think how brazen he was, how he got away with it.

On the way back from training, Roper would sometimes bring back meals from a Chinese takeaway in Gatley. We never went out for family meals in those days. We didn't have that kind of money. You would get a buffet at family occasions, christenings, with sandwiches, sausage rolls and the like, but not going out for a sit-down meal.

Roper would buy a banquet for five and the kids thought that was great. Then he would say: "I don't want to drive home." That's when he started to stay at the house. Gary had left by then to play for Wimbledon, and Roper slept in Gary's bed, in Paul's room.

Looking back now, you see the signs. The family from Boston, who Paul stayed with, used to send us letters all the time. We even got into the habit of exchanging cassettes, to catch up with each other. They spoke about what they were up to, then we recorded a message for them.

Their letters came in that old-fashioned blue Air Mail paper, which had the address on the front and opened out into the letter, without an envelope. It was one sheet of paper with the letter written on the inside.

I think they suspected something. In one of the letters, they wrote: *I just want to say keep an eye on Frank Roper with your Paul.*

I was not sure what that was about at the time, and never asked about it because I never dreamt for one moment Roper was abusing Paul.

Then the family came over for a game in Manchester. I met the mum, and again, she mentioned Roper and said that she was not sure about him. It was not a clear reference to anything, so I thought that she meant that Roper had been hitting Paul.

I asked Paul about it, worried Roper may have been using violence to make him improve his game. But Paul said: "Take no notice, Mam, I don't know what they mean."

That preys on my mind even now, more than 40 years later. Forty years too late. I realise that she must have been worried about Roper, had an instinct about him, but just could not be sure. But that is with the benefit of hindsight.

Roper kept hold of our Paul all the time while they were in America. That first trip he had just turned 11, it was a big trip for a lad of that age. I knew nothing of what happened over there at the time.

Gary was on the first trip, he was that little bit older, and I knew he would look out for his little brother. But Roper put him with a different family, in another house. We never knew, and there were so many times when there were clues, but not enough to find out what was happening.

If you look at what happened to our Paul, Roper threatened him, he would say to him, all the time: "I will kill your parents, your brothers…"

No wonder he did not say anything. I have only come to fully realise that in the last few months, since he did the interview with the *Mirror.*

That will stay with me forever, to my dying day.

•••••••

Looking back, I can see that Roper had drummed into Paul that he could not play with his friends and that he had to focus on football. Paul was so desperate to make it that he believed him – that was Roper's influence.

That time he came in crying, when he was upset and I knew that Roper was involved, and he said that he had hit him, when Roper turned up at the door, I punched him straight in the face.

It knocked him flying – Paul heard it upstairs. I told him: "Don't you ever hit my child. Don't darken the door again." But he still came back. He just would not give up. Paul said he wanted to keep on playing for Nova and wanted to keep on seeing Roper to make him a footballer. So we let him.

Years later, when he was about 40 and after all three children were born, Paul rang me out of the blue – it was really late and he said that he was coming to stay. I opened the door and practically had to carry him in because he had been drinking. He went to stay in the spare room, but then he kept dragging me out of bed.

He said: "I need to tell you something."

I said: "I'm tired and going to bed."

I thought he was going to say he and Bev were finished, but then he said: "Frank Roper abused me."

I knew he was serious because he was in such a state and I said: "Why didn't you tell me?"

He said: "I did not tell you because my dad would have ended up in prison."

I thought Roper had been hitting him physically, I did not realise it was beyond physical abuse. I have broken my heart over this. I wake with the same thoughts, I sleep very little as it is, but this is constantly on my mind.

I love all the kids to death, they are always on the phone checking we have everything we need, and this has really made us realise that you cannot take anything for granted. I know now what Paul has had to deal with right throughout his adult life. It has affected his career, his relationships, his marriage. He once threatened to go and live in Spain after he stopped playing – I did not want him to go, but he and Bev were having rows over his drinking, and I said that he should do whatever he thought was best for the two of them.

I am so proud of Bev, she has stuck by him all the way. He went to live in hotels when they hit hard times, and I said to her: "I don't blame you, I would not put up with his drinking." People would go to the house to visit them and he would walk out. She is a brick and I love her to bits. She rings all the time to make sure we are all right; Bev has been absolutely brilliant with us, and the children, she is a wonderful mother. Paul could not have got a better wife, she has stuck by him through it all.

•••••••

Paul has been much better since he did the interview and went public. I am really glad that he has come forward to tell his story, to help others, but also just to ease his pain from it.

His brother Anthony was very upset when he found out. He looked after Paul when Gary was at Wimbledon and, of course, he thinks about what might have been. We all do. But we had no way of knowing.

We went to Cornwall on holiday when they were both in their teens. We left Paul with Anthony and even then, Roper came around and Gary heard them arguing. Yet even then I did not see the warning signs. It is so hard. If he had said 'he has been hitting me' I would have looked into it.

I have never known the full extent of what Roper did because it would kill me. I see Roper's face in front of me when I go to sleep at night, and I think back to all the times he used to pick me up at work to go and get the things for his business. I am absolutely tormented by him even now.

Paul has struggled to show his emotions at times, but when his dad had a quadruple bypass operation recently and Paul came to visit him in hospital, I could see the tears in his eyes. There was a team around his dad, and he could not get his breath, and Paul had to take off on his own for a while, we did not even know where he went.

Even now, all these years after his playing career, seeing Paul walk out at White Hart Lane for the last game there, we think *that's my lad*. It took us back to Wembley and the '91 cup final. We have had so many happy memories, and have been lucky in so many ways.

We have such pride in all the family, Paul does not realise just how proud we are of him, and his brothers, because we never talk about it really. Some things go unsaid.

It's not just the football. Paul did not do any exams at school but he has taught himself Spanish and managed to work through all the things he needed for his business; he has done really, really well and I am so proud of him, I can't tell you. He is really good with us.

Bert has been a brilliant father and husband – I always tell him I would never leave him. He was strict, but it is hard with three boys, you have to be.

And through everything, Bev has been absolutely brilliant. Anybody else would probably have left Paul years ago; she is absolutely wonderful with him. They have three lovely kids – and now their first granddaughter, our great granddaughter – so it all worked out in the end.

I think Bev saved him; I am so glad that they came through it all, and found happiness again.

What happened to Paul still haunts me. Sometimes, when Bert gets up in the middle of the night, I end up thinking about it all over again.

I cannot get out of my head what happened then, to my own child. It has stayed with me, I talk about it with my family, friends, even neighbours. You never really get over it. For all those years, we just saw Roper as Paul's coach – trying to help him make it as a footballer. The truth is devastating.

Only a mother can understand.

I just hope, above all, that others learn from our story.

········

Dad's story

My name is Bert Stewart. Football has brought us some great times. Seeing Paul play for England at Wembley is something I will never forget; something I could never have achieved. I played cricket, a bit of football and liked boxing when I was young in Manchester, but that was about it.

To represent your country is an amazing accolade, and we had another great day out at Wembley for the FA Cup final in 1991. We were all there to see him, it was unforgettable.

Believe it or not, when they were growing up, Gary was probably the better player, as Paul says himself; he had more skill and ability, but was maybe a bit young to be in London by himself. Looking back, maybe he would have been better off a bit closer to home.

Paul worked so hard to make it. When he was at Blackpool, his coach told me that he trained so hard he was sometimes physically sick at the side of the pitch during the sessions.

Nobody bullied him or got the better of him when he was at his peak. I remember in one game, I think it was against Leeds United, he came up against Vinnie Jones who caught the back of his calf in a challenge. It looked like he might have to go off but I thought *that isn't going to happen*. Sure enough, there was another one on one and Paul made sure he got him back. Jones knew he could not mess about with him.

We went as often as we could to watch Paul play and the parents on the line used to drive us mad at times; they had no idea about the game, but still shouted the odds. When I nutted that coach, he had it coming to him. He was a disgrace.

We are very proud of all the kids, and so glad that Paul came forward to talk about what happened; it takes real courage to do that, but it has been a really positive thing for him, because he has been through hell, and has been carrying that secret for such a long time. He seems happier now.

We knew that people would blame us, that they would say we should have known about it, and the family knew there would always be those who had a go at him. The darts player Eric Bristow made a comment about the football sex abuse scandal and lost his job as a Sky Sports pundit – something he later apologised for.

You can understand how tough it all must have been for a kid of Paul's age. You cannot begin to think about what he went through. Bev stood by him when many would not have done and she has got him through it.

I would have killed Frank Roper if I had found out when he

was still alive. It is as simple as that, and I know that Paul understands that too, as do his brothers.

I could not accept it and I know there are some people who would say that cannot be right, that Roper had human rights, but it is evil, and he should have been strung up in my opinion.

Paul was worried I could have gone to prison if I found out, and he suffered himself as a result of that, which is my biggest regret. Roper told him that he would kill me, his mother, his brothers if he said anything, which is why he never did.

Despite the heartache, the happy memories stay with me.

We spend the winter months in Benidorm and stay at the same hotel every year. We love to chat to the other guests about football. Whenever I meet people, I always say: "My lad used to be a footballer."

They ask: "Who did he play for?" And when I say his name, "Paul Stewart," they always remember him.

We love all our family; we are very close to them.

Bev is absolutely wonderful with Paul, we have told her that. She saved his life, and we are so proud of them both.

Chapter/9

SECOND FAMILY

When I left Manchester to start my football career in Black-pool, it was my dad who took me. He had a car by then; a bit of a banger – an old Vauxhall – but good enough to get me the 50 or so miles from Cleeve Road to Bloomfield Road. When he dropped me off at the guest house where I was staying, it felt like the first day of the rest of my life. This was everything I ever wanted.

Because of what I had been through, living away from home held no fears for me. For some young apprentices, living miles away from where they grew up might have been a traumatising experience. Not me. I missed Mam and Dad, of course, but living in a new town wasn't daunting in the least. I felt a sense of freedom. There was no homesickness.

Escaping Roper was liberating but it wasn't like I suddenly reverted back to the happy-go-lucky lad I was before I knew him. In fact, I was still pretty moody and miserable. If I felt happy then I rarely showed it. I'd just blocked out what had happened to me and tried to bury it in the darkest corner of my mind. That was the easiest thing to do. I didn't realise that concealing my secret would come at such a price.

That wasn't the only reason why I was so moody. Right from the start of my football career, I put incredible pressure on myself to make it. Turning professional wasn't enough; I had to become a regular in the first team as soon as possible – and then I had to stay there. I knew how intense the competition for places was and I made sure I did everything to keep me in the coach's good books. I took nothing for granted. I'd do extra training whenever I could, just to show how keen I was. Throughout my career I always worked hard. It was partly fuelled by an inferiority complex. I never felt I was as good as the others and so I'd work my socks off to make up for it.

Pre-season training sessions at St Annes could be tough. The beaches by the old pier cafe – famous now for its giant chocolate eclairs – were beautiful, wide open spaces with the sands stretching for miles into the distance under leaden skies. Coaching staff had to hide in the dunes. During the long distance runs, some of the old-timers would try and hide there, then run out and re-join the pack.

In the early days, on those punishing sessions, back and forth up the beach, I sometimes found myself with the goalkeepers at the back. I was a kid among big men and it could be hard going. It could be bracing on the seafront.

I made my professional football debut on February 10th, 1982 against Rochdale. Blackpool were in Division Four. It wasn't a particularly memorable game but that didn't matter. I'd come a long way to get to this point in my life.

SECOND FAMILY

The following week the first team were playing away, whilst the reserves were at home. For some reason, I just presumed I was going to be in the first team squad, so I turned up at the ground ready to travel. I got on the first team coach, a spotty teenager sat alone at the back, waiting for the coach to depart.

We were just about to go when the manager – Allan Brown was in charge at the time – noticed I was on board. Imagine my embarrassment when he announced in front of the whole squad: "Paul Stewart, you shouldn't be on this coach – you've been selected to play for the reserves at Bloomfield Road." I don't think I'd ever been so embarrassed as I had to get off the coach red-faced in front of the rest of the lads. I can assure you I always checked the teamsheets from that day forward, which were posted at the training ground Friday afternoons.

I found the football comfortable enough but socialising with the first team squad was another thing. I wasn't a confident person; I didn't find it easy walking in to busy places, like a noisy dressing room. I'd feel self-conscious. The drugs would help with all that and more later in my career. For now, it was easy to keep my head down and concentrate on the football.

At least when I went out for a drink with the first team, the alcohol would ease my awkwardness. I'd drink pints at first when I went out, just to fit in with most of the other lads. It wasn't long before I ditched the pints and moved on to bottles. *Budweiser*, *Beck's* maybe. I still prefer bottles now. I tried other drinks but was violently ill after a night on Pernod and black-currant which I never touched again (and never will – the smell, even now, takes me back). But I generally enjoyed a drink, it helped me forget things.

It was on one of these nights out that a Blackpool girl caught my eye. I was out for a Sunday night drink in the Oxford pub in the town, an old fashioned boozer with a great atmosphere, busy most weekends. I headed there with the rest of the players on a regular basis as time went on – it was a real favourite haunt after matches. We would have a good night, talk about the game, share the ups and downs of the season. And, of course, meet the local girls.

When I spotted this girl, I was mesmerised by the fact she was with her identical twin, though I noticed they were not the type who dress exactly the same. I was still very shy, and had no intention of approaching her for fear of rejection. They were already attracting a lot of attention from lads at the bar.

She walked to the bar to order a Liebfraumilch, a popular drink amongst girls in those days. I could see instantly how good looking she was, with blonde hair and brown eyes. As she passed, I found the courage to say something.

"Hiya, love." That was the extent of my chat-up patter. Like something from the Boddington's advert. I had my jeans on and M&S cashmere tank top (all the rage then, hard to imagine now…) and she had a pair of dungarees, but they were shorts, because it was summer. "Hello," she replied, politely, before walking back to her friends with her sister.

A week later, I bumped into her again when I was out with the lads in a bar called *Rumours,* one of those '80s 'fun pubs', where they had bar staff dancing on the tables all night and a DJ.

It was one of the most popular places in Blackpool and became a regular hang-out for the players. There was often a big group of around about 12 of us there for what our manager Sam Ellis called 'team building'. It did work; we went out together all the time, because we did get on, and the teamwork started to tell on the pitch.

I plucked up the courage to go over and speak to her and she told me her name was Bev. The conversation flowed and we arranged to go out on a first date. Bev didn't have the first idea about sport and did not pretend to be interested when I told her I was a footballer. She couldn't care less.

She had been working since junior school days; at 11, she would help out in the hotels and B&Bs in Blackpool with her sister, they would call it slave labour these days. We were from very similar backgrounds and hit it off straight away; she lived on one of the biggest council estates in Blackpool, very similar to mine in Wythenshawe. I suppose I wasn't like your normal bloke who would regularly meet girls; I wasn't outgoing or chatty. But we still got on well. It felt like something completely new to anything else I had known.

I still joke about one of our early dates. I had booked a place called the Braithwaite Manor. I had a blue Pinstripe suit on, and Bev was a in a short mini dress, so we were both very smart for the occasion. It was quite a posh restaurant in those days and she could not make her mind up over the menu. Then we talked about the steak. I said: "What about fillet?" and she replied: "I don't like fish." We still laugh about it now. I had to explain what I meant and she has had fillet steaks ever since. That one bit of advice has cost me some money down the years.

•••••••

When I go out in Blackpool now, that team of the '80s is sometimes up on the bar room walls. It makes me realise just how young I was when I started playing; just out of school, just turned 17 on my debut, living away from home for the first time.

Many years later, I bought the Oxford pub as an investment – after I had retired as a player – then sold it on as a site for an Aldi supermarket; it was a very good business deal as it happens, so it has been good to me in many ways.

I could never have guessed it when we first met that this would be my partner for life. In those days, she never went anywhere without her sister. They both wore necklaces – Bev with *Beverley* on and Karen with her name on – and sometimes they would swap them around on a night out for a laugh, just to confuse people and have some fun.

Over many years, I have come to learn that it is true what they say about twins. True for these two anyway. Bev would call as Karen was just about to call her (without dialling a number, they would find themselves talking to each other as they picked up the phone to one another). They once bought exactly the same watch on the same day (on their birthday – the strange thing was, they were 250 miles apart, we lived in London and her sister was in Blackpool). When Bev fell pregnant with my son Adam, our first child, Karen had 'labour' pains. (Hard to believe, I know).

I think that I was still 18 and Bev was 19 when we met. Whatever the exact ages, we were very young really, but we bought our first house by the time we were 21, and she would come and see me at the digs where I was staying.

At the start I was with Betty and Alan Thompson, who have both passed away now. They were loved by all at the club because they looked after so many young players. 'Mrs T' for short, she took in kids for decades, including me and the likes of Trevor Sinclair, who also played for Manchester City and is now a TV pundit. She nurtured most of the talent that came to the club in those days.

I was earning £16-a-week as an apprentice; by the time I bought my first house with Bev, it was around £250 a week. So it was a real struggle to get on the housing ladder. We had to get a 100 per cent mortgage and we really did skint ourselves to make the payments every month. We were living 'over the brush' as they said in those days – co-habiting, and out of wedlock – as we tried to build our home together.

For a long time, we were saving up and when I moved out of Mrs T's, I went to live with Pat and Dave Serella – a former player at Blackpool, and a big mate of John Robertson, the Nottingham Forest winger, who was best man at his wedding. Bev would come around and stay. We just loved it there; we would laugh all the time with them, and their kids, I really felt part of the family. It was great to be free of Roper and the dark cloud I had been living under back at home in Manchester. I felt like I was leaving all that behind me.

'Robbo' – John Robertson – turned up once. Growing up, I had watched him in the great Nottingham Forest side under Brian Clough. I was starstruck. It was real hero worship. I was tongue-tied at first, not sure what to say. He had some great tales from his career. He told me how inspiring Clough was as a man-manager, and how he had helped him to turn his life around, on and off the pitch. I remember him always being able to get away from his defender, steal that extra yard with a little feint, a drop of the shoulder, to get a cross in.

Clough had re-invented him as a player. He told us that he

was going out on loan to lower league clubs, he went back up to Scotland to play for Hamilton for a while, and was on the way out before Cloughie arrived. He turned him into one of the best wide men of his generation; I will always remember watching him put that cross in for Trevor Francis to score the winner in the European Cup win over Malmo. Francis, the first £1m man. Robertson, the best player on the park. I was amazed to meet him in person.

Life with Pat and Dave was good craic. As an apprentice in those days, you earned so little money that you were expected to help out in the digs, show that you could be independent and look after yourself. I did some babysitting; Bev would come and stay, I was left in charge of the house when Pat and Dave were away and I tried to look after the place as much as I could. One Christmas, Pat came back to discover that I had put up every bauble and decoration she had ever possessed – it was like Santa's Grotto – which made her laugh out loud. She had not expected that when I offered to help with the Christmas bunting.

They had two sons. Mark is the eldest – he is 41 now, Daniel is 38 – but they were seven and four when I lived there. My 'adopted family' guided me through so much in the early days of my career.

I was just a young kid really when I started getting this fan mail, a string of letters from an admirer who I quickly learned was not a female penpal, but a man. He would send me bizarre cryptic messages like 'if you feel the same way about me, pull your sock down at the end of the game' and 'if you have received this message and understand, just pull your shirt out of your shorts at the end of the game.'

Of course, being a teenager, I would make an effort to avoid doing what was mentioned in the letters every week, especially after what I'd already been through. But inevitably I did forget and I would either pull a sock down when I was not meant to, or pull the shirt out and the messages would start coming in all over again. Pat and Dave, not surprisingly, became concerned that it might have been an obsessive stalker who would turn up at the house. I was not sure what to do. I knew I would never hear the end of it if the players found out I had a man writing me letters on a weekly basis.

So I decided that I had to tell the manager and in the end they called in the police. It was like something you would see on the telly; in the end, the police went out to see him and just issued him with a warning.

Bev really hit it off with Pat, and they confided in each other about any problems I had in those early days. Many years later, Bev would talk of her suspicions over my past and how it had impacted on me. Even then, right at the start of our relationship, she had seen the signs. Pat had no idea Frank Roper was involved, but my future wife was starting to put two and two together.

My old Blackpool boss Sam Ellis, still a great friend to this day, could see the 'potential' in me in those early days of my career. Attitude to him was as important as ability. That desire to be a footballer, there from such a young age, shone through. He jokes with me now: "You gave me the impression the only thing you wanted to do was to play football." But there was a serious side to it.

There was a tough lesson in an early league match against Port Vale at a cold, windswept Bloomfield Road. When the centre half Phil Sproston gave me an off-the-ball right hander, Sam was incensed. But he knew that I had to look after myself, and that was why he came running down from the stand. He saw me feed Phil the elbow, splitting his nose open to the fury of his team-mates. Strangely, given the circumstances, that was a 'pivotal moment' in my early career for Sam. Not being bullied by the big lads. Even just out of school.

I ended up scoring 56 goals in 201 games for Blackpool. It was an honour to be voted into their Hall of Fame alongside the likes of Stanley Matthews, Stan Mortensen, Jimmy Armfield, true legends of the game; the fans selected the names up there too, which means even more to me.

It is still a funny feeling when I see the old team photos. There I am, still spotty as a teenager, staring out – ready for the Panini album. Those days at Bloomfield Road gave me some laughs and helped me move on from a difficult time in my life. I was the most determined and enthusiastic footballer you could imagine and Sam was a real father figure as well as a tough, but fair manager.

•••••••

The one shadow from the past was Roper. There were so many times, when I saw him around the club, that I thought about going to Sam. Once I felt sick to the pit of my stomach when there was another young lad following him around at training. I just knew the reason.

A few months after I finally went public in 2016, I went to see Sam at his house in Treales, just outside Blackpool. He is retired now and enjoys the quiet life, living in a bungalow in the village. After a bit of small talk, I asked him about Roper. Sam would have known him well.

"Did you have any idea? Were there any clues at all?"

"The abuse never crossed my mind," Sam told me. "I wish now someone had said something to me, my youngest lad went on two trips to New Zealand and Thailand with Roper."

It was Sam's son Tim, at 13 or 14 years old, who was playing for Nova, Roper's team. Frank had asked if Tim could play as soon as he took over as manager in 1981. Roper had a big influence in the junior section of the club because he brought in good players. In fact, his players probably saved the club from extinction. Blackpool sold David Bardsley for £150,000 to Watford before they got £200,000 for me. We both went on to play for England.

Over a cup of tea, Sam continued: "He was a very successful scout. How it could happen with so many kids knowing – how do you keep so many quiet? It can only be fear. Fear of retaliation for talking, or fear they would not make it as a footballer.

"I've no doubt the main problem for all the victims was that it might bring their career to an end. Roper was well looked after at Blackpool, a prominent member of the club, he was always made welcome. But if you look at it from a football point of view, and think about what he did back then, his CV was immaculate. No one knew anything about it until you went public – and that was more than 40 years later."

To use his words, Big Sam was 'flabbergasted' when he found out. Roper's abuse of trust spread from Nova through to his work at Blackpool. It was noticeable how much the landladies used by the club for young players all loved Roper. The grooming process seen with my parents was extended to the women who acted in loco parentis to the young charges at Blackpool FC. They would tell the club how Frank went that extra mile to make the kids feel at home – taking them to the amusements, out for fish and chip suppers and so on.

Those in charge of Roper – and even the likes of the land-ladies – had no reason to believe it was anything other than him looking after them. And Sam was adamant that no one ever spoke to him about the trips to Thailand. No one raised concerns at the time.

"When Roper came back he had bales of goods for the shops, and that was supposed to pay for the trips. The lads used to serve there. One of the players with the junior side back then, his mother worked as his secretary. No one had any suspicions as far as we knew. If they did, no one came to us.

"I think women are sometimes more intuitive than blokes, but there was no sign, no mention of it. I have been through certain things in my head. There are certain things you cannot fathom. Frank Roper is one of them. I shared a flat with Gary Speed for five months. There are times, even now, when I am kept awake thinking *why? how?*"

Sam lost his youngest son Tim in a tragic road accident after he was hit by a lorry, aged 28.

He recalled: "At my son's inquest, it was accidental death. The lorry driver said it had just happened to him. There was a suggestion he intended to do it and people in cars said that, but the coroner said there was no way anyone could have been sure, so you hope for the best.

"It is hard to say now if there are some things you do not want to believe but as far as we can make out, there is no answer to why and how."

SECOND FAMILY

In the aftermath of my revelations about Roper, there was speculation that Tim may have fallen victim to him during his time at Nova, but Sam said: "I am clear that Roper had nothing to do with his death, and I am 100 per cent certain of that."

Typical of Sam, the thought that his decision to send his own son on the Nova tour of Thailand may have somehow influenced other parents; that still preys on his mind to this day.

I dread to think what he would have done, if I could have somehow summoned up the courage to tell him about Roper.

"You don't know what your reaction would be until you are faced with that problem," he sighed. "I really don't know if Roper would have got out of my office alive, what would you do if he is facing you there and you know that the kid is telling the truth, how would you react?"

I left the bungalow more convinced than ever that Roper had fooled us all. The club manager, the landladies, the parents – nobody suspected a thing.

••••••••

In the spring of 1986, Bev told me some news that would change my life forever.

"I've got something to tell you," she said as I walked in the door after training one day. "I'm pregnant."

Becoming a father wasn't something I had planned and the news came as a total shock to us both. I was 20 years old and still just completely focussed on making a career in football. The thought of having to look after a baby made my head spin though I was happy, of course.

The news didn't knock me out of my stride. In fact, if

anything, it helped me enjoy one of my best seasons on the pitch in 1986/87. I was knocking them in for fun and it started to get me noticed.

One of the clubs eyeing me up were Manchester City. City were still in the old first division – if only just. They were fighting relegation and desperate to find someone who could score the goals that would help them beat the drop.

Sam thought I could do it at the next level. "It's what you deserve son, it's a just reward," he told me.

It was the culmination of all the hard work we had put in together. He had taught me so much – and I really tried to put it into practice out on the pitch. When I left for £200,000 in 1987, he saw it as the next step in my career; he would never have dreamed of standing in my way. He was glad for me, even though he was losing his best player – someone who had scored 21 times that season.

I had been a few years with Blackpool and was starting to wonder if it was ever going to happen to me. I'd had some good times at the club. Sam had steadied the ship and led us to promotion to Division Three in 1985. But I wanted to better myself. I made my debut at 17 and I had seen players like David Bardsley move on before me.

There was talk of West Ham and Rangers coming to see me. But so much was down to how you played if the manager came to see you in a game. I was never seen as a prolific scorer as a forward, more a provider, my work ethic and creating chances for others were the biggest part of my game. They often said I should play up front with a regular goalscorer.

For our first meeting at City, I didn't have an agent. I took Bev across with me because I was so nervous, and just had a figure in my head for my weekly wage which I decided I was going to stick to. Negotiating my own deals was something I did throughout my career. I stood on my own two feet and fought my corner. It was also a sign that I had a decent business brain – something that has held me in good stead in later years. Knowing that I would soon become a father gave me an extra determination to get a good deal.

When I arrived at the old Maine Road ground, all the press had been tipped off and were there waiting for me. The photographers took me onto the pitch and before I knew it, I had a scarf in my hand. I was holding it up but thinking: *This is a bit strange, I haven't agreed terms yet.* Then, believe it or not, they sent me off for a medical. It was a case of going into the boardroom and *this is what we are offering, sign here.* Sam told me they had made a bid and clearly thought it was a done deal.

In that first meeting, I was introduced to Freddie Pye, a scrap metal merchant who was director, the coach Jimmy Frizzell – and the team bus driver called Derek. I remember thinking: *What the fuck is the coach driver doing here?'* (I learned he would sit on the bench, and got so involved in team affairs that he was invited to contract talks, he was into everything).

I don't know where I found the strength from but I heard myself speak up. I said that I wanted £450-a-week and they were offering £350. I also wanted a £10,000 signing-on fee, which was not a big amount even in those days.

They kept telling me 'this is an opportunity, you will be rewarded.' But they were offering 150 quid more than I was on at Blackpool, and I was going up three divisions. They would not agree.

Every time I spoke, they scurried through to the next room to

see the then chairman Peter Swales who was conducting negotiations by remote, from the other side of the wall.

I left without agreeing a deal, devastated, and the next
morning on the back of the *Daily Star* was the headline 'Greedy
Stewart'. I remember saying to Bev: "That is my chance gone."
Blackpool were due to get £200,000 for me, and they were not
happy because to them it was £200,000 down the swanny.

I had the same discussions in the same room with the same
people – including Derek the coach driver – a short time afterwards, and still we could not come to an agreement.

Then Blackpool were playing away at Northampton, I scored
a hat-trick, and when I went down the tunnel, City legend Tony
Book was there with Jimmy Frizzell. They said: "We're going to
give you what you are after." I signed the next day.

It had taken three weeks. But I had stuck to my principles and
at last, I had my big break. United were my team, though I had
never mentioned that in any interviews for the papers. There
was no hesitation because of any rivalries there.

As far as I was concerned, I had worked hard to get this opportunity. My relentless pursuit of football success was a way of
dealing with the restless anger inside me. It gave me a channel
and a focus. I'm sure that team-mates must have thought I was
just determined and single-minded. To outsiders, I must have
appeared like a regular young footballer chasing his dream. I
just thought that it would be enough to bury my secret; to block
it out. It was the natural thing to do and a part of my life I
didn't need to think about.

Making it big in the game was all that mattered. Moving to
Manchester City was my big chance, and I could not wait to
take it.

Chapter/10

LOOK BACK IN ANGER

When I eventually signed for Manchester City – after all the issues with the deal – the right back John Gidman placed an empty briefcase by my side and said: "There is your signing on fee" on my first day at the club.

It was a reference to the fact I had been to the ground on three occasions for contract talks before I finally agreed terms in March 1987. I suppose it broke the ice – I was exceptionally nervous – and Giddy, as we called him, was one of the great characters in the dressing room who made me feel at ease with his joke.

I think we had very few games to go in the old first division when I signed, and our fate was already sealed by the time I arrived at the club.

Whilst the first team squad boasted some experienced players; the brilliant winger Peter Barnes, midfielder Neil McNab, centre back Mick McCarthy and Giddy, we also had some youngsters who had just broken through, and that season in the top flight was just a step too far for them.

The likes of Paul Lake, David White, Ian Brightwell, Paul Simpson and Steve Redmond were all brilliant prospects, but in a struggling side.

I didn't set the world alight in my first few games, but I was finding my feet in the top flight after playing my entire previous career in the lower divisions.

Inevitably, relegation came with just 39 points won and, as is the norm, a new manager was appointed, or, in this case, a new coach. City didn't sack the old boss Jimmy Frizzell; they moved him upstairs as General Manager. They then put a young coach from Norwich City, Mel Machin, in charge of first team affairs.

Machin raised a few eyebrows at one of his first training sessions when he got us to shout out 'Sid', 'Jack', and 'Fred' as code names for certain things you had to do with the ball. If you wanted it from another player, you would perhaps shout 'Sid', if you wanted someone to leave it, you'd yell 'Jack' and maybe if it was a back heel, it would be 'Fred'. It turned training into a bit of a farce and some of the older lads just took the piss. The worst thing was we had to persevere with it and use these code names in matches.

During the close season Machin's first signing was another striker, Tony Adcock, a player I had come across in the lower leagues, who had a great goalscoring record at Colchester. With myself and the lightning-fast Imre Varadi still at the club, I knew one of us was going to be surplus to requirements.

I returned from the summer break and Mel soon made it clear that it was Imre and Tony who were his first choices. Rather than accept it, I got my head down and trained really hard.

I was determined to make my move work, and, either by luck or fate, Tony Adcock picked up a knee injury in the first few weeks of pre-season which meant that Mel had to play me on the up and coming tour of Sweden and Norway.

I started hitting the back of the net straight away. Everything I touched turned to gold, so much so that when Adcock became fit, Machin couldn't leave me out.

That season in the old second division, I was on fire and ended up scoring 30 goals in all competitions – the first time a striker had done that for the Blues since the former Manchester United and City legend Brian Kidd.

I hit a hat-trick in one game, a 10-1 win over Huddersfield Town – Tony Adcock and David White also got trebles; Neil McNab scoring the other. They were playing in what became known as their 'bruised banana' kit. They left Maine Road battered and bruised, and all of a sudden I was idolised by the City supporters. As a Mancunian, I became a fans' favourite, especially with the die-hards in the Kippax End. In interviews, I avoided talking about my childhood allegiance to United.

My parents Joyce and Bert were still living in Manchester, as were my brothers Anthony and Gary. Anthony and my uncle Brian, both life-long City fans, were over the moon, watching me week in, week out, banging goals in, and accompanying me to the sponsors' lounge almost every week to receive man of the match awards.

I would have a drink in the bar back then and enjoyed seeing my family. I got on well with the senior pros, and the young lads, and we would have a few beers together in the club bar. But it was not like London, and the night club days at Spurs later in my career. Despite the thriving music scene in 'Madchester',

Factory Records, the Hacienda, Happy Mondays and all that, my 'rave days' were yet to come. It's funny looking back to think that I gave the music scene a miss when I was in the city of my birth. I would make up for it once I got to London. This was my first big break in the game; playing at the top level. I knew that I really had to apply myself to make my mark.

Leaving Blackpool also meant that I finally left Roper behind me. I was so focussed on football that even when I went back home to see the folks – they were still living in Cleeve Road – Roper was banished from my thoughts.

In the butty shop run by my mum, I would pop in after training and the local kids loved to see me there. It was like being a local hero, for the first time, and as a young player, I really enjoyed that.

The papers were speculating on which clubs were going to sign me; it just seemed that I couldn't put a foot wrong. City wanted me to sign an extension on my contract, and I had agreed to do it after we returned from a break in Bournemouth. One evening I had been out with Barnsey, Giddy and Neil McNabb, and we returned to the hotel a bit worse for wear and headed straight to the hotel bar for a late one.

A stranger approached us – I was unaware who he was at first – but it turned out he was a club sponsor who had been out for a meal with the City directors.

After he had shaken hands with the other lads, he was introduced to me, and when he realised who I was, he blurted out: "You're the lad Aberdeen have just bid £750 grand for."

Next morning, the director Freddie Pye pulled me to one side and asked if I was going to sign my new contract when we got back to Manchester.

I told him: "I've had second thoughts and, as I still have a year or so to run, I'm in no rush."

Of course, upon my return to Maine Road, the manager got me in and the contract had been improved. Talk about being in the right place at the right time!

When I was at City – and bear in mind, it was my first full season for them – I was told there were a number of big clubs after me, including Rangers. I got a message asking if I would be interested in playing for them. Because of my problems at City, especially with chairman Peter Swales, I said that I was. They wanted me as a replacement for Ally McCoist.

Then I picked up the paper and saw that Graeme Souness was looking at Mark Hateley in Monaco the following weekend when they were supposed to be interested in signing me and I thought *what is going on?*

I had reservations and by then I knew Spurs were in for me and Everton as well as Rangers. Even shortly after signing for City from Blackpool, at that very early stage of my career, I quickly learned how the money side of football worked.

I did not have an agent because they were asking ten per cent of what they got on your contract in those days and I just did not think it was worth it.

I went into every negotiation with a figure in my head – and stuck to it. It had almost cost me the move to City early in my career, but it seemed to work. When I was offered a new deal following the Aberdeen bid, I realised they were securing their asset, and they were unaware someone had leaked that bid to me.

After that prolific first season at City, I was told that Manchester United were in for me, and that Alex Ferguson was ready to make an offer. But Swales said to me: "You are not going over the road, over my dead body." He had many faults, but was City through and through. He could not face the idea of selling his free-scoring forward to their arch rivals.

•••••••••

I would clock up a lot of bookings during my City days. To be honest, it was nothing new. I'd developed disciplinary issues during my time at Blackpool. I was banned for the opening two City fixtures because of a series of bookings for Blackpool. The same would happen when I joined Spurs.

I had a very short fuse. If players fronted me I would be more than up for a showdown.

Blackpool manager Sam Ellis would get annoyed – and rightly so – if I was booked for arguing with the ref, or kicking the ball away. But he encouraged me to use my weight, height and physical power against some of the hard lads we faced week in, week out.

I knew I had anger inside me. Having Roper around the club at Blackpool did not help matters. Every sighting of him at training, or at the ground, brought it all back. Whenever I noticed him with the kids it was especially hard to take. He was there on matchdays as well, lurking around the directors' box, in the stand. My brother Anthony saw him at one of the home games at Bloomfield Road, early on in my professional career.

Once I left, he used to bring in kids to sit with him and watch games, such was his position of power and trust at the club. I have only learned that since going public, and it is hard to fight the feelings of sheer anger and frustration even now.

I carried that rage on to the pitch at City. Some of my tackles could be X-rated at times. I was never afraid of getting stuck in as a kid but as I got older I often crossed the line. I enjoyed the buzz of sliding into an opponent or using my strength. Football was a physical game back then, a lot more than now, and it was a part of the game that I could take to extremes.

Looking back now, I feel sure that some of the anger seen by others – and reflected in my disciplinary record – was the aftermath of my childhood. Trying to come to terms with it all was not easy; the fury inside was a result of me trying to compute all the things going on inside my head.

I wish that I had tried to address those issues back then, instead of later in life, and had looked at counselling. It is always best to seek help as early as you can. Even when I addressed the issue of my drug addiction later in my career, I did not touch upon the anger and the abuse, that aspect of my past; instead, it stayed locked away.

I think that is also why I appeared arrogant at times, distant; I found it hard to open up, and that was almost an image which became hard to shake off as I got older and moved around the game.

Over the course of my career, there were many trips to appear before the FA disciplinary committee at Lancaster Gate in London. I was summoned there year in, year out. You might get away with the odd season of bad behaviour but if it was repeated – that was deemed unacceptable. I would be called to explain myself and give my side of the story. Then I would find myself banned...again.

Some of the bookings were often for dissent. I didn't always have the best of relationships with referees and towards the end of my career I developed such a reputation that I would be shown a yellow or red card even when I didn't deserve one. It depended on the type of referee you had sometimes. Some would engage in banter and some would just throw the rule book at you. I remember running alongside Roger Milford once and sniping in his ear: *You're fucking shit, you.* Straight away he would fire back at me: *Don't be getting on at me because you're playing shit.*

I'd let players know what I thought of them from time to time. For me, it was all part of the psychological battle that you had to win. As a forward you might have to deal with a defender in your ear. Sometimes the best way was not to respond but on other occasions, you had to nip it in the bud; let them know that you were not going to put up with that kind of thing.

When I dropped back to midfield later in my career, I had to face the likes of Roy Keane, Steve McMahon and Bryan Robson, who all loved a battle.

Keane rarely spoke a word to me, but it made no difference. He had the ability to get wound up all on his own. I certainly never engaged in any 'sledging' with him during the '91 FA Cup final because I was so intent and focussed on keeping him out of the game. That was my job and I was determined to do it. It was the key task for the final, what Terry Venables asked for in the run-up to the biggest match of my life.

But the league games were a different matter; I was the instigator and would often be trying to wind Keane up from kick-off. Forest were real rivals to Spurs at that time and Keane, Stuart Pearce and Nigel Clough were like a band of brothers; they all looked out for each other.

I remember Pearce saying to me: "He is twice the player you

are mate" talking about Clough, when I got him sent off for the only time in his career. But that was fine by me. I knew I had got to 'Pyscho' and the needle just added to our encounters. With Keane, he did a ridiculous second challenge on me in one match, when he was already in the book, so he was obviously going to be sent off. The Forest lads must have hated me.

Another player I'd clash with would be Steve McMahon at Liverpool. We even got in to a fight in a testimonial – for my future room-mate Stevie Nicol. We had been on at each other all game, even though it was supposed to be a friendly. We ended up exchanging a few punches next to the tunnel at Anfield before we were separated. Some bad feeling had spilled over after we had clashed in league games.

You also knew you were in for a battle against the likes of Tony Adams and Martin Keown at Arsenal. I enjoyed a centre half who would come and kick me and I gave as good as I got.

Alan Hansen never kicked me once – but read me like a book. With Stevie Bruce at Man Utd, and Adams, you knew how to handle the physical side of their games. Hansen was a Rolls Royce of a player, always two steps ahead. If I kicked him, I would get a booking and again, he would end up on top. He was the best centre half I ever played against. It was a shame he had gone by the time I arrived at Liverpool. He was sheer class when he was a player.

My Premier League record, with Liverpool, then Sunderland, suggests that the leopard had not changed his spots even in the final years of a playing career that stretched back more than 18 years, from my debut with Blackpool at just 17. I had 10 yellow cards, and two red, in 56 games (including subs appearances) although my reputation did sometimes go before me.

At least the football was giving me a channel for my aggression. All my emotions came out on a pitch; it felt like I could be myself without thinking about what I *should* be doing.

When that was taken away from me, when my career came to an end – it was then that I started to struggle. There was nowhere for my anger to go; it would swirl up inside me and I would take refuge in drink and drugs or take it out verbally and in the way I behaved on the ones I loved.

••••••••

A matter of weeks before I moved to City, my son Adam was born. February 28th, 1987. A date I will never forget.

I was up all night when he was born and words couldn't express what I felt when I held him in my arms.

He was finally delivered in the early hours of the morning; 12 minutes past three to be exact at Blackpool Victoria Hospital, after which I joined the team as we were playing away at Port Vale. Without having any sleep I insisted on playing and scored a hat-trick.

Over the course of the first full season at City, we decided to get married. There was no romantic proposal, it was just a decision we both came to because we wanted more children and believed we should do things properly.

But even as I prepared to marry Bev, in June 1988, Frank Roper was in the background. She became aware of my determination not to invite him.

As you might expect, questions were asked at the club because the wedding was in Blackpool, Bev's hometown, at the registry office, and Roper was effectively Chief Scout at the club.

We were still good friends with so many people connected to Blackpool, including 'Mrs T', who loved Frank, and she wondered why he wasn't coming to the wedding. When Bev was making all the arrangements, I made it crystal clear I didn't want him around.

We had our evening do at The Imperial Hotel on the seafront and I did everything I could to ensure he didn't appear unexpectedly at the door; I could just imagine him turning up with a slimy grin, clutching a gift and a greetings card. *My congratulations to the happy couple.* I wanted our wedding day at least not to be tainted with any unhappy memories. Bev sensed there was something more to my determination not to invite him but she just did as I asked her.

Aside from Roper, there were other distractions threatening the happiness of our big day.

We were due to get married on the Saturday and on the Tuesday before, I met with Terry Venables, by then Spurs manager, who wanted to take me to join him in London. The pull of the North West was strong for me as by then, I knew that Bev would struggle if we moved away from home. She loved having her family around her in Blackpool and obviously my family was in Manchester.

But it was hard not to be excited by the Tottenham interest, so I went down to London to see Venables. I got the train down in the morning and met him at the Royal London Hotel in Kensington. It was a nice hotel, very plush, and as I walked in he was sitting in the lounge having ordered champagne for us both. As the ice-cold bubbly slipped down my throat, he gave me his patter; about how Spurs were going places and if I signed, I would be a big part of his plans. It was all very enticing. Venables knew exactly how to treat a player and tell him what he wanted to hear.

Once again, I didn't have an agent, but I did have a figure in mind for what I should be paid. We discussed the financials and Venables seemed happy to agree to my terms there and then. With the expensive champagne now drained from the bottle, he asked: "So what do you think, Paul? Will you give it a go? It will be a great move for you?"

It was hard to say no. We shook hands on the deal, which to me was as good as signing a contract. I headed back on the train buzzing in the knowledge that I would be stepping out at White Hart Lane come the start of the 1988/89 season. As a footballer it was a great move for me; though I wasn't sure Bev would share my excitement. As I said my goodbyes to Venners at the Royal London, I told him: "I don't want this getting out, I am getting married on Saturday, I don't want anything to spoil Bev's big day."

Two days later, on the Thursday, Everton got in touch with Manchester City and made an offer. I felt it only right – out of courtesy – to go and meet their boss Colin Harvey. I told him what the contract entailed at Spurs and he said straight away: "We can't match that."

In hindsight, what I should have done was say: "No worries, I am on my way." Instead, Harvey said he would go and speak with the Everton chairman. I waited there for hours, and after what felt like an eternity, he said: "Right, we can match it." I did not agree to anything, but asked for time to think it over, explaining that I was getting married in two days' time.

Granada Reports, no doubt aware of this battle to sign me, turned up at the wedding. I am still not sure how they found out about the ceremony but they were there as we walked out as man and wife for the first time. Fortunately, they did not ask me about the transfer. I explained to them about it being Bev's day, and they were great. They just did a story on our wedding instead.

The next weekend, I officially signed for Spurs. Colin Harvey went on TV. He was very unhappy, suggesting that Everton had been used to up my money.

Of course, I knew that was not true. But there was little I could do by then. I signed for a club record £1.7m, one of the highest fees ever paid by an English club. For a day, a full 24 hours, I held that record.

The next day, it was taken off me when Spurs signed a certain Paul Gascoigne, one of the hottest properties in the game, for £2.2m. He had been at the centre of a real battle for his signature, with Liverpool, Manchester United and Spurs all going to the wire for him. In the end, Terry's charm had worked its magic yet again.

The bright lights of London beckoned for us both.

Chapter/11

HOME ALONE

After a quick honeymoon in Cyprus during the summer, I had moved down to London on my own. The club was obliged to put me up during the first three months of my move until we found a house, so they sorted out a room in the Swallow Hotel in Waltham Abbey. Gazza was staying with me as he'd arrived at the same time.

Bev travelled up and down from Blackpool as much as she could at first, but it wasn't always easy and she couldn't stay too long. It meant that me and Gazza were often left to our own devices. Sometimes, we were joined by other players. At one stage it was me, Gazza, Steve Sedgley, Nayim and Paul Walsh staying in the hotel. We would get up to all sorts of antics. It was a case of *right, we have finished training, what are we doing tonight lads?* It was like a holiday camp at times; you can say it encouraged team morale, but there was a down side.

After training, we'd head back to the hotel early afternoon, have something to eat and maybe use the hotel's leisure club for a sauna or a swim, maybe a massage.

By the time we'd done that, it wasn't even tea-time and a long night stretched out in front of us. So we headed to the bar to kill some time. The alternative was staying in our room, lying on the bed and flicking through the channels on the TV.

Drinking soon became a daily routine. Pretty much every night we'd find ourselves perched on the hotel bar stools with a *Holsten Pils* in front of us. That only changed when Bev was visiting. We were on it virtually every night. Bottles of lager with maybe the odd brandy if we were in the mood.

It hadn't been a great start to the season for Spurs. Right from the off, it seemed like the 1988/89 campaign was going to be problematic. On the morning of the season opener at White Hart Lane, the club was forced to call the game off. The powers that be had decided at the last minute that construction work on the newly revamped South Stand meant the stadium was 'unfit'. The authorities took a dim view of that and later docked the club two points.

I'd received a six-match ban due to yellow cards picked up during my time at Maine Road. It meant I had to wait until the start of October before being included in the team. In the meantime, we'd won only one of our four league games – a 3-2 win at home to Middlesbrough – and had lost by the same scoreline to our bitter rivals Arsenal at White Hart Lane.

Perhaps it was no surprise with new players coming in and some big names leaving. Venables had shelled out a lot of cash in the summer of 1988 but he must have recouped a lot too. Clive Allen was sold to Bordeaux; Steve Hodge left for Nottingham Forest and also heading out of the door were Nico Claesen (Antwerp), Neil Ruddock (Millwall) and Tony Parks (Brentford). Ossie Ardiles also left on a free to QPR. Despite that, we had plenty of top class operators in the team – Chris Waddle, Gary Mabbutt, Terry Fenwick, Paul Allen, Paul Walsh; all very talented players.

I was itching to get involved and named on the bench for the visit of Manchester United on October 1st. Illness to Waddle gave me my chance – he'd turned up at White Hart Lane with a fever and though he started, he couldn't finish the game. I replaced him, trotting on to the pitch wearing the number 12 shirt.

It was very close to a dream debut. The teams were locked at 2-2 heading into stoppage time. I burst into the penalty area and was brought down as I closed in on goal. The referee pointed to the spot. I could be a cocky individual on the pitch and so I went over to our regular penalty taker, Terry Fenwick and snatched the ball off him. I didn't care. I earned the penalty and it was a chance to break my duck and become an instant hero.

I put my right foot through the ball and hit it well but with the keeper diving to his left, my heart sank as I saw the ball clatter against the crossbar. A chance blown to win the game. The boss absolutely slaughtered me in the dressing room. "What were you thinking Stewart? You cost us the points there," he told me in front of the team. I won another penalty in the next game against Charlton but this time, of course, Fenwick was back on spot kick duty. No questions asked.

Instead, I had to wait until early November before getting my first goal. It came after just six minutes in a home game against Derby County, courtesy of a Waddle cross. Gazza was first over to congratulate me; he was clearly delighted for his mate, grabbing my head in both his hands and giving me a trademark toothy grin.

Waddle, the creator of my goal was phenomenal that season; he would end up going to Marseilles for £4.5m, a British record at the time, finishing the campaign as Spurs' top scorer.

As for me, I wasn't setting any houses on fire, despite my opening goal on November the 5th. The goal wouldn't have lived long in the fans' memory being the consolation in a 3-1 defeat. It was a poor start to the season and was our fourth defeat on the run. Bought as a striker, scoring goals was the issue, and I soon started to feel under pressure. There was an easy way to deal with that – work harder on the training pitch. And go on the beer.

●●●●●●●●

During that first season, I received a phone call from Bev when she was on holiday in Lanzarote with her friend – Bobby Mimms's wife. She told me she was pregnant again.

It felt more important than ever to find a family house so I could move out of the hotel. We found a property to rent in Broxbourne, a quiet, pretty place not much more than half an hour's drive from White Hart Lane. Then, not long after, we moved into a lovely detached property in the village, which backed on to a river.

Moving down south was a big change for Bev. She was already bringing up Adam and now she had to prepare for the arrival of our second child, away from her mum and twin sister and everything she'd known. If she wanted to see her family, it would involve a long train journey back to Blackpool.

It was a big change for me, too. The playing style at Spurs was different to anything I'd previously known.

HOME ALONE

I was adjusting to players of such quality. I almost felt that I was not good enough to be on the same pitch as the likes of Waddle and Gazza. I decided that I had to work my socks off to make up for the inadequacies. Sam Ellis taught me if you think you have worked hard in training, or on the pitch, work harder. That stayed with me throughout my career. It was an important lesson in life.

I also felt that I needed to get to know my new team-mates, so it was important to spend time with them. So even when we moved into the new house, I still went out drinking on a pretty regular basis. Bev would be stuck at home looking after Adam, who would have been about a year old.

Venables kept me up front despite the barren spells, and I wanted to try and repay him. I took a strange decision in the end. Despite everything I had been through during my teenage years, I turned to God.

There was the most beautiful church in Broxbourne and I decided to pay a visit. There was a man who lived next door – I am not sure now if it was the vicar, a parishioner, or church warden, who had the job of keeping an eye on the building – so I knocked and asked if I could go in. Adam was christened there, it was in a stunning setting. Even though I am not deeply religious, I was having such a bad time that I started to go every Thursday after training.

The man next door would happily give me the key to go in there alone and I used to just sit and pray. It was a time to consider everything in life; my future, the demons of the past, the performances out there on the pitch. I did not ask to score goals. Instead I would ask for the family, for Bev, and Adam, just a toddler, to be happy. And that was it, just some little things for others. Some people might say it is a coincidence, but my career soared. Did the Lord provide? I will never know!

Towards the end of the season, I found the net on a fairly regular basis. In April, I scored in a 3-0 win at home to West Ham and then again in a 2-1 win at Wimbledon on the same day as the Hillsborough disaster, which put everything in to perspective. Just before the month was out, I scored a hat-trick in a 5-0 thrashing of Millwall. I finished the season with 12 goals.

With things looking up, there were more nights out. Then it wasn't too long before pre-season kicked in: Ireland, Scotland, Norway and Spain during the summer of '89.

Gary Lineker was big news at the time. He had just joined us from Barcelona and he scored his first goal for Spurs against Cork City at Musgrave Park on the trip to Ireland.

In the build-up to that game, we told the boss that we were going to take Gazza fishing. It was before Italia 90 so he was not at the peak of his fame but he still loved to get away from it all. Of course, it just turned into an excuse to go for a drink.

We were in Mayo, in the west of Ireland. We called a taxi but when the guy turned up to give us a lift, I thought: *He's absolutely steaming drunk,* which is never a good quality in a driver. He was determined to give us the full tour and to get us to the three pubs in Bohola.

There is a famous song about the place:

There's three pubs in Bohola, as everybody knows
MacDonald's, Clarke's and Roche's,
where the craic like honey flows
And lovely Mary's here with me, I never more will roam
Mayo how I love you, Bohola my dear home

HOME ALONE

He was giving us all the patter about the local sights and told us 'Jack Charlton fishes here' – which I suspect you might get everywhere you go in Ireland. Then he said: "Let's go to see my mum first." We thought *you what?* but I think she must have been expecting the entire Spurs team – there was a massive spread of food, which was very good of her.

Her son then wanted to take us around the famous 'three pubs' where everyone was desperate to get their photo taken with Gazza. We were a bit of a sideshow really, but it was a great laugh. By the end of the afternoon, we were all legless but we knew we had to go back to the team hotel for the evening meal.

The taxi driver/tour guide had been drinking with us through the afternoon and we asked him: "Are you sure you are going to be able to drive us back?"

"Sure, no bother," came the reply before he took another gulp of his drink. We just laughed.

Then we thought: *What about the afternoon angling? The boss will be suspicious...*

We came up with a plan to stop at a fishmonger's on the way back, where we bought a frozen trout. It was so obvious we had not caught it – it had been gutted – but we took Gazza down to the river for a photo and hooked the fish on the rod. He was beaming with his prize catch. It was *the one that didn't get away* and indeed had not been away anywhere for some time – apart from a freezer compartment.

It was clear for everyone to see what we had been up to, but we took it back to the team hotel anyway. I am sure nobody believed us but it was such a funny story that they all just went along with it.

On the Norwegian leg of the pre-season tour, I received the good news I'd been waiting for. We were having a team meeting when the boss broke off from talking tactics. "I'd just like to say congratulations are in order for Paul," he told the squad. "His wife has given birth to a baby girl." Chloe Jade Stewart was born on August 9th, 1989, at The Queen Elizabeth Hospital in Welwyn Garden City. The day before she was born, I scored in a 5-1 win over Viking FK.

Some family travelled down to Broxbourne to help Bev after Chloe was born. But it can't have been easy looking after a young son as well as the baby.

I knew she wasn't happy and although I wanted to stay at Spurs, I contemplated a transfer back home. The thought crossed my mind of going to Everton, due to it being so handy for Bev, her folks, and my family.

In the end, after about 16 months in the Broxbourne house, we decided that I would stay in London and she would head back up north. Adam had been going to a playgroup in London but we agreed that it would be better if he started school in Blackpool.

I knew it was the sensible thing but I also knew I would miss my wife and my young son and daughter. It was another upheaval which made life at Spurs difficult. Bev was just 18 or 19 when we met on that fateful night out. She has always stood by me, even when the job has taken me hundreds of miles from home. I knew she and my two kids were happier in Blackpool, but the emotional support they gave me was taken away. I found that hard.

I tried to make sure I travelled back as often as I could to Blackpool. When the new season got under way, I'd head back up north after the game at the weekend, unless I had to stay for treatment on an injury.

I remember making those long journeys from London back to Blackpool.

All the way back, on the near-five hour motorway drive, I would practise telling Bev how much I loved her. I would rehearse it in my head, a simple thing. When I arrived, it never happened.

Instead of saying what I felt, she would open the door and I'd find myself saying something insulting. *Alright. I'm tired, I need to sit down. Have you put on weight?*

The aftermath of the abuse, the impact, was still with me. I was still struggling to express myself. I would find it hard to express the emotions which were a given for others, the simple pleasure of saying you love someone. I'd get by without having to be honest about the way I felt, but it just meant that I was simply blocking things out. The drink helped with that. Or at least I thought it helped.

········

When Bev went home, I moved into a house with Gazza in Dobbs Weir. Gazza stayed with me throughout his time at Spurs, right up to his move to Lazio. Gazza was an unusual character right from the off. He was never nervous about playing; he cost £2.2 million but he did not see that as a major issue because he was such a good player.

Off the pitch, he was a strange combination; shy, but a real practical joker; one of the brightest young talents in the game, but so insecure as a person; generous, funny, apparently happy-go-lucky, but riven by strange habits, doubts, medical conditions, quirks of character.

In the early days, if we went out for something to eat together, he would finish off his main meal then he'd order three desserts and make himself ill. I never understood. It was hard for me to know even what to say. I had not seen anything like that before. It became an every day aspect of life with Paul Gascoigne.

Gazza's first girlfriend from school, Gail Pringle, came down to be with him. They lived in Dobbs Weir together first, while we lived in Broxbourne.

There used to be a phone on the team bus in those days and he would go down to check where Gail was and what she was doing as we made our way back to London after an away trip. One of the lads picked up the phone upstairs to listen to his conversation once, unbeknown to Paul. He was checking on her movements, asking what time she would be home, that kind of thing. Controlling her night out by remote. The relationship did not last.

I was also with him the night he met Sheryl. It was clear he was completely besotted with her from the start. But he treated her just like his first girlfriend; he was very demanding.

All was not as it seemed with Gazza; you would think he did not have a care in the world; he became one of the most famous faces on the planet at Italia 90, and those tears in the semi-final, yet was so insecure in his relationships.

Every day he would be up to something causing havoc with his jokes. I got on well with Steve Sedgley who later joined us from Coventry City and who we both knew from the England youth and under-21 set-up. He was nicknamed 'Long Neck' for obvious reasons.

HOME ALONE

One day, whilst Venners was taking training, all the players were on the pitch in a circle around the halfway line. Gazza was late. As always, the boss was asking me where he was, like I was his minder. Just as I was about to make an excuse, Gazza turned up with someone alongside him, carrying a brown sack.

The sack was moving as if something was in it, and just as Venners was about to rollick Gazza for being late, the bag was opened and an ostrich ran out wearing a Spurs shirt. There was a number 7 and SEDGLEY written on the back. The lads just fell about laughing.

This ostrich was running around our training ground in a white Spurs shirt, with the whole team watching. Everyone, the kids, the training staff, the apprentices, stood open mouthed or in hysterics. Venables' face was a picture.

The bird went running off in a panic and he had some job getting it back. I am not too sure what the animal rights people would say if they knew that Gazza had a bird from the local zoo dressed in a Spurs shirt loose on the training ground. He claimed that he had 'borrowed' it from Broxbourne Zoo. We were never able to verify if that was the case.

On another occasion, there was a fanatical supporter who came to watch us at the training ground every day. In his 40s and dedicated to the cause, his name was John – and Gazza used to rib him all the time.

One day, Gazza turned up in what can only be described as a camper van, like a box vehicle with ladders which go up the back. It looked like an old-fashioned *Oxford* van, or one of those 'recreational vehicles' you see in the States. Gazza put a traffic cone on the top and said: "Look at what the lads have done there, John. Will you get that cone off for me?"

Keen to please, John climbs up and quick as a flash, Gazza jumps in the front and floors the van, the accelerator pressed down as far as it would go. John's legs are hanging off the back and he is shouting: "Please stop, you are going to kill me."

Gazza brought it to a halt and John managed to get off without any serious injury. John always seemed to fall for Gazza's tricks, pranks and practical jokes. It was beyond dangerous but he was such a fan that he didn't mind, any way just to be involved with us and he was happy.

At home, Gazza's behaviour was just as bizarre. He was showing the first signs of his obsessive compulsive disorder. If we were driving to a game together – which we often did, as we were sharing a house – he would tap the rear view mirror all the time because it had to be exact, precise for him. He had to do things his way.

On other occasions, no matter how important the match was, he would want to return home. It could be Manchester United, but he would make me turn back checking if he had locked the door, or if the remote for the TV was in alignment. He would go upstairs to the bathroom to see if the towels were straight.

One day, we were running really late for a game. I was driving to White Hart Lane on the A10 and he said he had forgotten something and insisted we go back, which meant driving the wrong way down a dual carriageway.

He had a wallet with a flap where he kept his credit cards. He was holding this wallet up in the front seat, pretending it was a police warrant card while I was flooring it because we were so late. We were meant to be at the ground an hour before the games but we were so late they had already been on the phone asking where we were.

The bulimia also became more and more frequent; he would make himself sick after a meal all the time. It was a condition which was not well known at the time, before even Princess Diana had spoken out about it.

As a young lad from a working class background in Manchester, I did not have a clue what was going on. He pulled on his stomach muscles to see if there was any fat underneath the skin. I was too young to be able to comprehend what it all meant, but that was Gazza.

There was one occasion when we were staying in the hotel when Gazza ran up a £25,000 bar bill. I wasn't around but apparently he had invited all his family around to stay and then left the club to pick up the drinks tab.

Venables took us to one side and asked us to explain what had happened. Paul wasn't bothered. There were some mini milk cartons on a tray and he spent the time ignoring the boss and firing them over at a few of the press lads.

Instead, the boss directed his questions to me, as often happened. "What's been going on – how are we expected to pay this?" As if I could do anything about it.

Gazza could be friendly, generous to a fault, but fame could lead to trouble. And often through no fault of his own.

One time, quite early during our time together at Spurs, he came up to Blackpool for the opening of *Lineker's Bar*. He was on crutches from the injury sustained in the cup final and we were asked to go to the opening night as a favour.

At the launch night, two lads came up to Paul and asked him if he would buy them a drink – but he explained he was not going to the bar because he was on crutches. Next morning at 9am there was a police officer at my door saying two men had reported an altercation with Paul. One of the lads claimed the two of us had beaten him up and broken his jaw.

I told them: "Nothing could be further from the truth, Paul is on crutches." They still took Paul into one room to be interviewed, and I had to go into another to face various questions about the night before. You would think that common sense would have told you Gazza could not beat up someone on crutches. But he still had to go through a police interview, albeit an 'informal' one at our home.

It turned out the lads who had gone to *Lineker's* had left, gone down the road, got drunk, with one hitting the other in order to sell the 'Gazza brawl' story to the papers.

Paul was being set up; and it did make him paranoid about strangers at times, in my view understandably so.

•••••••••

Gazza's eccentric behaviour continued long after the Spurs days. He rang me one Friday night after I had finished playing – my daughter Chloe was still at school, it was around 2001. I used to go out on a Friday with my mates, so I turned the phone off. He called about eight o'clock at night.

I did not phone back, then at 8am when I turned the phone on again I found I had been bombarded with calls from him and messages on the answerphone saying he was coming to Blackpool to see me. Then there were a series of messages asking: 'Where do you live?'

Around lunch-time, he arrived and I said: "How did you find me?" He got someone to drive him up to Blackpool from London, and went into the *Tesco* down the road. He just went in and started shouting: "Does anyone know where Stewy lives?" Unbelievably, there was a mate of mine in there who saw him and said: "I know it is North Park Drive but I don't know the number."

So Gazza came to the top of the street, looking in windows to see if he could see any photos of my kids on the mantelpiece. One poor fella found a slightly drunk Gazza looking through his window first thing in the morning shouting: "Have you any idea where Stewy lives?"

When Gazza eventually turned up at my home, it was a lovely summer's day so we had a BBQ in the back garden. For a bit of fun, he started going through his phone ringing up famous people. Eventually he got through to Robbie Williams and made him sing his hit *Millennium* down the phone to Chloe and her school friend, who could not quite believe it.

Chloe recalls Gazza encouraging her to cycle down the drive, while he waited at the bottom to stop the traffic in case she came onto the road. He tried to take a photo. It didn't work, so he just threw away the camera. He was full of fun, full of laughs, a great fella just to be around when he was on form. But he was also completely unpredictable, hard to fathom, and a nervous wreck at times.

When he was ringing random people on his phone, he could not get through to TV presenter Dale Winton. So he left a load of abuse on his answering service because he didn't answer straight away. I am still not sure why he had the number for Dale…but that was Gazza, totally unpredictable and capable of doing anything at any time.

When he went to the World Cup in Italy in 1990, he would call to tell me about his progress. He said he was forced to try and get some sleep ahead of the last 16 game against Belgium but he thought he ended up putting in his worst performance of the tournament. So, the day before the quarter-final against Cameroon, he went out into the heat of the day and played three sets of tennis.

It reminded me of the time at Spurs when there was a game at Portsmouth. Gazza got up in the middle of the night and played three sets of squash before going back to bed. When Terry Venables found out, he hit the roof. Gazza's squash opponent was dropped from the squad. But he played. The trouble for Terry was that Gazza was performing so well on the pitch, it was impossible to drop him.

Just before the World Cup in France in the summer of 1998, Gazza was with the England team and I went up to meet him at the Mottram Hall Hotel near Manchester. I think it was the final game of the warm-up and he wanted to see me.

They were going to pick the squad the next day. I met him in the bar, but I was driving home and he was not drinking as he had a game. Then David Seaman came down and said: "The gaffer – meaning Glenn Hoddle – wants to see you." Seaman suggested he might be in a spot of bother. I think they had assumed we were drinking in the bar, but we were not. I left in the car to drive back up to Blackpool. It was just a social call, seeing Gazza for a big game to see how he was.

It has been well documented what happened next – Gazza wrecked his room when he was told that he had not been picked. Hoddle said he could not trust him – it was not a matter of his ability, but he could not take him to a big tournament without that trust. Yet when I left, Paul genuinely thought he was going to the World Cup.

HOME ALONE

There was a definite suggestion that they suspected he was drinking in the bar with me. But that was not the case. It was another example of Gazza being misjudged, just because of who he was, his reputation. He got desperately down about it at times.

Often, I could relate to his problems, which is why we got on so well.

●●●●●●●●

After Bev went back home, I had spoken to Venners. "I don't have a problem with being at Spurs, Terry," I told him. "But if a club up north comes in for me, could you let me know?"

I had started the second season at Spurs positively. I scored with a header from a Gazza free-kick in the first game against Luton. But it was a false dawn. I had to wait until the end of November to find the net again.

It was an up and down season which picked up in the final months. In March 1990, I scored the only goal of the game against the eventual champions Liverpool. Then a solo effort against Coventry was hailed as the Spurs goal of the season. We ended the season in third place in the First Division; I was second top scorer with nine.

Lineker, of course, was top scorer and he proved what a quality player – and person – he was. On one occasion when there was crowd trouble and fans broke on to the pitch, he was over telling them exactly what he thought.

During the summer, we went with Gazza and Sheryl for a summer holiday at *DisneyWorld* in Florida. We were staying in a resort hotel, and we went on all the rides together. Sheryl's daughter Bianca came along, but even then, Gazza would be fighting for Sheryl's attention. Bev was uneasy about it at times.

Then, with another summer over, I was separated from my family again as they returned to Blackpool.

The goals would dry up that next season, though a Venables master-stroke solved that. When one of the midfielders went off injured during a game at Luton, it was between me and Gary Lineker as to who dropped back. Obviously it was me.

Bizarrely, everything seemed to come right. I scored both goals in a 2-2 draw. I resumed back up front the next game but before long I found myself in midfield again and this time it was permanent.

I was happy enough. I was alongside Gazza – and anyone could play with him and look good. We were told to give it to him, even if he was just three yards away.

It may be that my new role in the team took some pressure off, at least for a while. I knew Bev and little Adam and Chloe were so much happier back home with all her family around her in Blackpool but deep inside, despite all the laughs with Gazza, there were times when I felt lost and desperately low.

I could come home from another night out and find myself in the darkest of places, questioning whether it would be best to end it all, wondering if it would be easier for my nearest and dearest if I was not around.

Chapter/12

ON THE EDGE

After Bev returned to Blackpool with Adam, I couldn't help but feel that I had been abandoned. Left on my own. It is a feeling I have since learned is common to many abuse victims.

It is irrational. You know that it is not based in reality. But you can't help feeling like that, especially when no one is around. It is a feeling you cannot put into words. That's when the drink – and later on, the drugs – came in. I was looking to fill that void, to escape feelings of loss, even though, when I thought about it rationally, that inner turmoil was not based in reality.

I didn't realise it then, but I had started to suffer from what I now know is depression. It would become a life-long affliction. Dark moods would come over me for reasons which are really difficult to explain. It is a silent but debilitating illness, and has hit me at various times over the years.

It does strike when you are at your most vulnerable but it is not an illness that happens in a matter-of-fact way. Only if you have suffered with it can you truly understand the feeling of despair, of loneliness, how you question the meaning of life itself.

In my case, it usually crept up on me like a dark cloud coming over the horizon; I knew the storm was on the way but I was powerless to stop it.

Over the years, it has manifested itself over a period of days, to the point where I am unable to manage the thoughts that enter my head. I can do nothing about it. It is not like a bad day at the office or feeling blue about everyday things; these are emotions which we all face at one time or another.

When I first started to suffer with depression, it was a state of mind which I could not fathom out.

It affected my sleep and that obviously had an impact on how I was feeling during the day. No matter how tired I felt, sleep became impossible for me as my mind ran riot with any problems in my life, some real, some imagined, driven by angst and my state of mind.

Most days I could handle them, sit down and work them out; but with depression, rational thinking becomes non-existent. There is no timescale on how long it lasts, or the severity of the attack. And it has no levels; it strikes at random and can stay for days or hours.

Generally, I coped with it by trying to be alone.

That life-long inability to discuss my problems, open up about my feelings, meant it did not seem possible for me to seek help. At its worst, suicidal thoughts became overwhelming; I could see no light at the end of a very dark tunnel.

I have contemplated ending my life on several occasions.

It is a dreadful feeling. The darkest thoughts start floating around my mind. I think about people being better off without me.

These are the completely irrational notions which I have to fight. The key for me is to think about my immediate family, and how they would feel if I were gone.

It is like the dream scene with the James Stewart character George Bailey in the classic film *It's a Wonderful Life.* I have to contemplate the worst to realise how wrong that would be, how hard it would hit all the people I love. I say to myself: *Paul, look at all the good things in your life.*

I should have addressed it through medical help or counselling when it first started all those years ago as a young man at Spurs; living on my own and struggling to find a settled home life whilst coping with the pressures that came with being a famous professional footballer at a top club.

It was a vicious circle. The abuse may have been at the root of my depression but so was the inability to express my emotions and find a solution to my problems.

In those early days of depression, at Spurs, when I was living on my own in London, I would make the wrong decision and go down the wrong path as I attempted to numb the pain or just find a happier state of mind.

There was the bliss of the escape, the oblivion that drugs used to bring. But I soon discovered that the altered state of mind only lasted for a short while. Once whatever I was on started to wear off, the 'down' was ten times worse than the feeling before.

I should have been enjoying my career. I was playing for one of the country's top clubs. I had money. I had a family that loved me, even though they lived miles from me. It seemed like I had it all.

Yet still the demons returned to haunt me, all part of the aftermath, the legacy of childhood abuse. Even then, I know there are bound to be those who would find it hard to understand what I had to be depressed about at the height of my playing career.

Depression started to be a major issue in my life during those Spurs years. It was probably at its worst when I gave up the game at 35.

It is a big part of my story; how I managed to overcome those dark times.

Chapter/13

HERO

Saturday, May 18, 1991

Wembley Stadium. Tottenham Hotspur v Nottingham Forest. The biggest game of my life. The biggest game of any footballer's career back then. The FA Cup final.

Gazza, our best player, our talisman, a man at the peak of his worldwide fame and talents, is down again. *He looks hurt.*

The game's not long started and he has already escaped injury and a red card. Going in for a 50-50, he's so enthusiastic to make his mark on the game that he has left a right boot in the chest of Ian Woan.

Now he's down again after a yet another reckless challenge on Gary Charles just outside the penalty area. He lies flat on his back, head in both hands as our physio John Sheridan attends to him. *It doesn't look good, it doesn't look good.*

The atmosphere is so intense in a cup final. You are surrounded by sound. You can hear the other players on the pitch but the nervous tension, the weeks of build-up, the sheer weight of expectation, zaps your energy. I feel drained already and the sight of Gazza lying flat on the turf is sapping me further. I can feel my blood turning colder. *Get up mate, whatever you do, get up. We need you.*

It's tough losing a big player in a big game.

An instant injection of confidence for the opposition.

Psychologically, they have one up on us.

I look around my Spurs team-mates and I can almost see their shoulders droop. Like an invisible weight has dropped from the sky. I can almost hear their thoughts, the same as mine, echoing around their heads: *We are done for now, Gazza is injured.*

I think back to the semi-final against Arsenal. Gazza's goal, that amazing free-kick. Ten yards out from the penalty area, dead centre. One step, two step, a long run up then bang! Right foot. Top corner. Seaman helplessly clawing the air. Absolute genius. The fans go crazy. Samways gets to him first and we jump on him. The early goal set the tone for us to beat our biggest rivals on the biggest stage of all.

This is now Gazza's final, his Spurs swansong before a move to Italian side Lazio. It can't end like this.

He is up. Doesn't look comfortable, but he's up. He can play on. He jogs gingerly back to our wall. Free-kick. Stuart Pearce takes it with that deadly left peg of his. He hammers it perfectly, our keeper Thorsvedt has no chance. It arrows into the top corner of our net. 1-0.

Gazza jogs back to the halfway line. If he runs in a straight line, he's okay. But before long he turns. He's down again. His face contorted, reaching down to his leg. The stretcher is called for. Venners is getting Nayim ready on the sidelines. Gazza has to go off.

HERO

I remember then, the clearest, truest, strongest thought I think I've ever had. *I have been through a lot to get to this day in my life, I am not going to let this take my chance away.*

It was not just about the pain of the abuse, not just about Roper, and what he had put me through, but the whole journey to become a footballer. I was not prepared to accept defeat.

This was the pinnacle of the dream I had followed for so long. Ever since I was a young lad. It had consumed me and enabled me to survive. The FA Cup was *the* competition in those days, like the Champions League final today. Every aspiring young footballer wanted to play in it; real *Roy of the Rovers* stuff.

I remember as a child being glued to the TV from as early as 9am, the BBC cameras filming both teams from breakfast, the pre-match meal and the team coaches travelling to Wembley, players doing interviews, trying to explain the euphoria of being a part of such a massive day in the football calendar. Little did I know that there would come a day when it would be me up there on the screen.

Everyone involved with the club had been on a high after winning the semi-final. As players, everybody wanted a piece of you: there were the media interviews, magazine requests, TV, the manager gearing up for the final by resting players in league games so that they were fresh for the big day. Cameras followed our every move as we got measured for our suits.

Then there was the obligatory cup final song – with Chas & Dave, of course. *It's lucky for Spurs when the year ends in 1*, so the song went. Doesn't feel lucky now. Gazza off after just 15 minutes, and it's about to get worse.

•••••••

My mum is at the game as is my dad, my brother Anthony, with his wife Gillian, and my uncles Brian and John. There is a whole Stewart entourage up in the stands.

But one member of the family is missing. Gary. The brother I shared so many kick-arounds with on the patch of grass in Cleeve Road cannot be there. In fact, as the match goes into extra time, he is on a plane; oblivious to everything.

Gary is desperate to know the score, to find out how his little brother is doing in the biggest game of his life. He even asks the captain. Anything to get some news from Wembley.

He has just won the league as a player with Witton Albion. They are on their way to Magaluf to celebrate. Something that had been planned for a long time. The last thing he heard before boarding the plane was that Forest were one up…

•••••••

At Wembley, everywhere Roy Keane goes, I follow. Venners says to me before the game: "If you can mark Roy Keane, follow him everywhere, stop him playing – we have a chance." As soon as the ball goes to Keane I am on him; I stick to him like glue. As I player, I will do anything I can to get an advantage. With Keane, I know which buttons to press. It seems to work. As the game progresses I get more space.

The second half kicks off. Then we have a chance to equalise. When the ball is fed into me, I turn and slip it through two Forest defenders to put Lineker clear. He rounds the keeper and is brought down. Penalty. *This is it…*

But Lineker does not score. Mark Crossley dives to his right and pushes the ball away. *Maybe it's not going to be our day.*

Keane goes over to Crossley and congratulates him. *I must keep going, we must not give up.*

Then, in the 55th minute of the game, it happens. Paul Allen picks up a hopeful punt from Nayim and strides forward towards the Forest goal. He slides the ball into me.

I check my stride. I am in the Forest penalty area as defenders race to close me down. I see the goal before me. *Keep it low, hit it hard. Keep it low.* I put my right foot through the ball and see it fly into the bottom corner.

The feeling is indescribable as I blow kisses to the Spurs fans going wild behind the goal. Lineker grabs me. *Thank you, thank you, thank you,* he says. Even an England hero and captain feels the tension on cup final day, and Lineker is no different – especially after missing that penalty.

●●●●●●●●

The quiet of the Princess Grace private hospital in Marylebone is in sharp contrast to the fevered tension of Wembley. Gazza is given a room with a TV and ensuite bathroom on the third floor. It is an upmarket private hospital with guests paying £230 a night but that's no consolation to Paul. It is only two months since he was last here – to undergo a double hernia operation.

Soon he will undergo a two hour operation to treat his cruciate ligament injury. The injury every footballer dreads.

The next day, he will be plastered over the front and back pages of the newspapers. 'Gazza's £13m Own Goal' will scream the *Daily Mirror*.

It is a reference to the fact that Lazio president Gianmarco Calleri has suggested they will now call off the transfer which would make him the richest footballer in Europe. He says: "We are now satisfied that this cannot happen and we will pursue other objectives." Gazza won't play again for at least six months.

•••••••

Extra time at Wembley. Pat Van Den Hauwe sends a long ball into the Forest area. Walshy is on as a sub. He gets his head to the ball and it loops over Mark Crossley and on to the bar before Stuart Pearce puts it out for a corner Walshy puts his hands to his head. We exchange looks in the penalty area as if to say: *Is this second goal ever going to come?*

We do not have long to wait. Nayim swings in the corner and I get my head to the ball, just trying to glance it on. Gary Mabbutt is at the back post. The next thing I know it is in the net. Des Walker buries his head in the turf. Own goal. We are in front for the first time.

We play keep ball, stringing together the passes before the ball slips under my foot. The tiredness has well and truly kicked in. But Forest are tired too. I get the ball again and feed it forward, then with the ball at Walshy's feet, the whistle goes. Pure relief. We have won the FA Cup; every boy's dream.

I will never forget scoring that goal, watching my shot hit the back of that net; the goal which gives you a little place in history. In a final, it is a dream come true. What topped it all off was winning the Man of the Match award.

There is now a photo montage in my office with the highlights of the day. The staff gave it to me to mark my 40th birthday, and it is alongside various mementoes and shirts bought at charity nights down the years.

On one of the photos, as we are lined up before kick-off, you can see Princess Diana talking to me with Gazza in the foreground beside me.

Gazza is shouting: "Where's FA Cup ears?"

He could not see Prince Charles, who we had been told would be meeting us before the game with Diana.

"Paul, can you please shut up?" I was telling him.

Princess Diana asked me: "Are you nervous about the match?" and I replied: "Not as nervous as I am about meeting you" and she smiled. It was true, as well – there was something about her, she had a common touch, and it was a real privilege to meet her – even with Gazza shouting 'where's FA Cup ears?' as she came up the line!

That final still stands out as the biggest game of my entire life, the one I will never forget.

We had started our FA Cup campaign on the first Saturday in January at my old stamping ground, Bloomfield Road. As we neared the stadium, I banished the ghost of Roper from my mind. There were other positive memories. I recalled the days when I was making my way in the game on £25 a week, building a career for myself free of the horrific experiences of my teenage years. I got a decent reception from the fans, which made me feel good.

It was a bitterly cold day with a fierce gale whipping around the old ground. As I stepped off the coach, I knew the Blackpool fans were sensing an upset: *We've got a chance to do them here...*

The game was a right old scrap. They hit the post and there was a couple of goalmouth scrambles but a touch of Gazza class made the difference in the second half. When he curled a free-kick deep into the penalty area, the ball broke loose on the edge of the six yard box. I turned and made enough contact with my left foot to see the ball bobble into the back of the net. It was enough to get us through. We survived.

At Wembley, I caught up with Bev not long after Gary Mabbutt had lifted the trophy. She did not see my goal because she was so overwhelmed that Rod Stewart was sitting just three seats behind her! Even the FA Cup final with all its hype didn't appeal to Bev. She had zero interest in the football.

We went straight from the ground to the hospital to see Gazza. Venners asked me to take the trophy in for him because we were so close. He was so happy to see us.

I remember Gazza asked the consultant: "Can I go to the party?"

"Not if you want to have a career!" he replied.

The boss made a speech and paid tribute not just to Gazza but the rest of the team for their never-say-die spirit when we were really up against it. The next day there were pictures of Gazza with the trophy in the hospital bed.

Steve Sedgley and I would continue to go and see Gazza as he recovered in hospital. On one occasion Gazza told us George Best had just been in to see him, and he was in a nearby bar.

I was a big United fan and he was an all-time hero. The last time I had seen him I was aged 11, and he was coming out of a lift in the US. I got Best to sign my cap for me. It was sad to see him going from bar to bookies, even then. He cut a sad figure, having a drink by himself, but I thought it was a nice touch going to see Gazza in hospital; he lived close by, and wanted to check and see how he was doing.

It was a ridiculous 24 hours after the final.

HERO

We went back into central London to the team hotel on Park Lane and my parents, Anthony, Gillian and my uncles were all there. We'd posed with the cup in the players' bar at Wembley after the match and they got to see me with all the players. It was great that they were a part of it.

The big post-Wembley party went on all night. Then we had to get up at 8.30am and take the coach from central London to White Hart Lane and the local town hall for the parade.

I remember seeing Freddie Flintoff three sheets to the wind in Downing Street after the England cricket team won the Ashes. It was the same for us on the bus. Most of the players were struggling from the night before, but it was still a great day. It was a fantastic atmosphere, a sea of fans out on the streets and we made the most of it.

After the final, we went on tour to Japan as part of the deal taking Gary Lineker to Grampus Eight. They took us for a week to Waikiki Beach in Hawaii as part of the celebrations for winning the cup. We were on the lash all the way. After a week at a top hotel on the beach front, we had to head off to Japan to play in the tournament.

We had to stop in America on route and ended up in a bar at LA Airport where Mitchell Thomas and Vinny Samways – or Vinny *Sideways* as we called him when we were winding him up about his safe passing – fell asleep on one of the seats. There was a last call for the flight. Should we wake them up or have a laugh and leave them? We left them.

They missed it and of course they were not very impressed by the time they got to Hawaii. They had to wait a day for another flight. We were sat on the beach when they finally turned up and the language was not the best!

The tournament in Japan had the likes of Vasco da Gama from Brazil and teams from the country's own top league. I remember travelling to Kobe and they were dumbfounded at seeing a Westerner, never mind a professional footballer from England. No one spoke any English and we were like aliens to them. It was such a different culture, a different world, but an incredible experience.

The performances on the pitch were not the best. We could barely pass to each other we had been celebrating so much. It was a mad summer, they were incredible times.

When it all eventually died down, I found the old feelings had returned. I had to find another way to lose myself. I was at the peak of my career, a Wembley hero, but within months I would find myself on the slippery slope to drug addiction.

Chapter/14

COCAINE

The first night I tried drugs, I had booked a hotel in central London, The Swallow International. They had a manager back in those days who would let us stay for free.

We checked in early, got changed and then headed out around a few pubs for a drink. It was always a good feeling going out on a Saturday. Home games or matches in the capital meant any night out would start in good time.

The banter was lively and as the pubs started to wind down, there was no chance of heading for home. Instead, we piled in to a taxi that took us to one of the city's big dance venues; thick smoke hit the back of my throat as I walked in; strobe lighting and laser beams illuminating crowds of happy party people hanging over balconies and waving their hands to a pumping beat. In the early '90s, house music was the big thing. And you got the impression everyone was on something.

Later on that night, I was stood alone. One of the DJs came up by my side and passed me something.

"Do you wanna try this?"

It was a pill with a smiley face. I recognised it as an ecstasy tablet or 'E' as it was known.

I cannot for the life of me remember why I thought it would be a good idea to take it. You think of everything I had to lose, and it was an insane decision. But there was a constant anger inside me, despite the success. This seemed like an escape.

Taking a swig of lager, the pill slipped down.

Almost immediately I thought: *This is it*. It was a feeling of euphoria. Everything suddenly seemed so good.

I fitted in with the scene around me. I was alongside young kids who probably spent time on the terraces at White Hart Lane and were so off their tits they had no idea there was a Spurs player in front of them. It wasn't about pure hedonism for me, it was a way of neutralising my feelings.

I lost myself in the music and when I was offered a wrap of cocaine later that same night, I just thought to myself: *why not?'* It just seemed like a great idea by then. What a combination. It meant that I was so wired I could not even go to bed that first time, I just kept on going.

Back at the hotel, I hit the mini-bar. I found the drugs enabled me to keep drinking without ever feeling too drunk. Sleep just didn't seem like a good idea. The night was a blur. I had no rest whatsoever, not so much as a 30 minute nap.

I carried on drinking as the sun came up. Then, with the mini-bar drained around lunchtime, I jumped into a taxi and was out again, meeting the lads in Hampstead Heath for a few more drinks. More bottles of *Pils* with David Howells and Steve Sedgley.

We were all in casual gear, out for a quiet drink. But as we downed lager after lager, we suddenly thought it would be a good idea to go to the PFA dinner at the five-star Grosvenor Hotel by Hyde Park, a popular haunt with actors and movie stars. There were cameras everywhere. The entire England squad was in attendance.

When we rolled out on to the pavement from yet another cab, the team coach pulled up. Then England manager Graham Taylor got out, followed by the players. I remember David Howells, who was pushing for a call-up at the time, taking it hard. He put his head down as soon as he saw the bus, and muttered: "That is my chance gone."

It was one of those situations where someone says in drink 'let's go to the PFA do' and instead of them saying 'don't be daft', we all just headed straight there. I was, of course, still in my Spurs tracksuit from the day before and still under the influence at 7pm on the Sunday night – having been out for 24 hours solid after the Saturday match.

When I met Peter Reid in the bar, he saw what I was wearing, and just said: "Fucking class." Everyone else was in their monkey suits, white shirt and bow ties. We must have looked a sight.

The doormen hadn't turned us away, but we did not have tickets so we could not get into the actual dinner. It was the stupidest thing to do to go to the event. For years afterwards we would say: *Why did we go there?* The answer was that we thought we were invincible. Especially me.

When the awards do came to an end, we all piled back to the Swallow Hotel so we could keep drinking in the bar. There, we saw David Butler, the Spurs physio waiting in the reception and I said to the lads: "We'd better avoid him." I was well gone by then, but alert enough to know the state we were in.

As the night wore on, I would eventually come down and my

body started telling me that I needed sleep. When I woke up, I just resumed normal life, feeling none the worse.

That was my first time – and I had got away with it. None of my team-mates seemed any the wiser at training. As far as they were concerned, I'd just been on a booze bender.

Discovering drugs the first time was like unearthing a special secret; I thought I had found the answer to the darkness I felt inside.

It wouldn't be long before I'd be out drinking again. In the loos of the bars and clubs we used to go to, people would say 'do you want a line?' If only I knew what it would lead to.

••••••••

I don't need to tell you that drinking and drugs were not a good combination for a footballer. I didn't become hooked on coke straight away but it soon became a big part of what I would do on a night out, often in combination with ecstasy; a welcome release from the way I was feeling.

To the outside world, I seemed fine. But I was very good at hiding the pain inside. I'd had good practice. Can you perform at your best when you have all that hidden and you are using the drink and drugs to handle it? I don't think so.

It is such a shame that my big chance with England came at a time when my old problems – the issues from my childhood – plagued my thoughts, especially any time I spent alone.

Even when I met up with the Three Lions squad for my debut, I had been out drinking all day; when I got to Bisham Abbey to meet with the full England squad for the first time, I still went straight to the hotel bar. We were not training that day – we usually met up Sunday evenings as we had all played on the Saturday – but after I checked in, I thought nothing of going down for a drink with a few of the other lads. Even though I was not alone by any means, you look back and think: *Was that right? What was I thinking?*

I had three games to prove myself, if you like, and Graham Taylor was a good guy, a fair manager, for all the stick he got later on in his England career.

I soon got my first full England cap. I felt like I had made it.

I went on against West Germany in the old Wembley on September 11th, 1991. A few days earlier, the newspaper back pages had reported on my new contract with Spurs, which allowed me to spend more time at home and to commute to training during the week. The new deal put an end to a potential move back to Manchester City.

I was very proud to win an England cap; I later played away in Russia and Poland. But the debut at the old Wembley just felt special, everything you had ever dreamed of as a young lad. It was over in a flash; the 66th minute came and my number went up on the board along with Paul Merson, the Arsenal midfielder also making his debut – and battling demons of his own, as it turned out.

Germany were still such a good side. It was hard to get anywhere near the ball. I got booked after I elbowed Lothar Matthaus, the German captain – that was my claim to fame from my debut. They won 1-0 and were better than us, full stop. It was a very rude awakening to life at the very top, on the international stage, even after all the glory of our cup final run, and the semi – and final – at the old Wembley. The Germans were simply world class.

My dad Bert, uncle Brian and brother Anthony were in the 80,000 crowd. Anthony had taken time off from his job at the Post Office and did not get back home until 3am; but he was proud as punch of his little brother, and it was great knowing they were there for me.

My dad was bursting with pride. He came to almost every game I played in and he loved the England days. He was funny. Loyal to the last, Dad never saw me have a bad game. I did not need to see the marks out of 10 in the paper to know when I had a bad game, any honest player knows when they weren't at their best. But Dad would blame everyone else in the team. Either they did not pass to me or they were not getting the ball to me fast enough.

My mam Joyce was fiercely protective, too. She had to stop going to my games in the end because she just could not take anyone having a go at her son. She was a nightmare if she heard anyone say a bad word about me in the stands.

At Blackpool, there was a group of lads having a go at me for being 'soft'. She confronted them and said: "Wait outside the changing rooms at the end of the game and our Paul will show you how soft he is!" I would come out and there would be three lads there, taking her up on the offer.

It was not unknown for her to go and see Sam Ellis and give him a real piece of her mind, including advice on his team selection. It would be fair to say it usually involved me getting a place in the side. He used to joke, shake his head, and say: "She is a bloody nightmare!"

I was lucky enough to gain England honours at every senior level. I came on against Scotland for England youth, then played for the under 21s, at B and senior level. I did not get into the under-16 schoolboy team because Paul Rideout was ahead of me.

When you joined up with England, they put you in a room with a player from your club if they could. I was usually with Gary Mabbutt. After the Germany game, I played for the England B team against France at Loftus Road, QPR's ground, in February 1992.

All the England lads thought I was going to move up to the full England squad, which I did for the friendlies against Poland and Russia later that season. I scored against France, and was thinking about that back at Bisham Abbey as I lay flat out, going over the game in my mind, when I heard a thud and realised Gary had fallen in the middle of the night. He was covered in blood from his nose, breathing but non-responsive.

I called the England club doctor at about 3am. Gary had to inject himself three times a day with insulin for his diabetes. He was changing from a certain type of insulin to another type and he had gone into a hyperglycemic coma. Had I not been a light sleeper, I am not sure what would have happened. Whenever I see him now I joke 'I saved your life' – I was not in a deep sleep and was reliving the game, and I am glad I was.

I've got immense respect for Mabbsy. It is incredible how he managed the condition to stay at the top level for so long. The lads would say 'you need sugar, you need sugar' because you could see the change in his character if his blood sugar dipped. He usually managed it so that did not happen, but he had to be so careful. Gary was taken to hospital, for check-ups, and was very grateful for my help.

Playing for England was what I always aspired to. But it did have its downsides. You went straight into a scenario to be told when to sleep, when to eat, when to turn up for dinner; it was all so regimented, and I am sure some players thought *here we go again.*

Back then, ex-Southampton boss Lawrie McMenemy was in the England set-up. Appointed as assistant manager to Graham Taylor in July 1990, after Bobby Robson's tenure as boss came to an end, he took the under-21s as well as helping the senior squad. All he seemed to be bothered about was whether your room was tidy. I felt we were being treated like schoolboys. Like me, many players had their own kids, it was not like they couldn't think for themselves.

After those three friendlies in 1991/92, my England career stalled. As that season progressed, the drink and drugs started to play more and more of a role in my life.

I just never seemed to consider how things looked. By that time, I was drinking heavily between games. And now I had also started to take drugs, the issues were magnified.

I was making excuses about not going home to Blackpool to see Bev. It would be 'treatment for an injury'; a team meeting; extra training. This was usually a lie, a simple excuse to allow me to do what I wanted. Many a weekend in London turned into a lost weekend.

Once the match was out of the way, free time followed a pattern. If we were away, there would be the full a la carte service on the Spurs 'five star' team bus. You got a selection of wine with the meal, then the *Holsten Pils* would come out. No wonder Spurs got the 'champagne Charlie' and 'southern softy' tag whenever they went up north. It was a three-course meal on the bus back to the stadium, like a proper restaurant.

There was often a few beers in and around Hampstead, as

many of the lads – including my big mate Steve Sedgley – liked the bars around there. Then we would often head into London, the bright lights, and a club, maybe a rave.

We would be making plans to go on the lash even as we hit the motorway, on the way back from the south coast, from Birmingham, wherever. Paul Walsh knew people all over the capital, and he was often ready for a big night before we got off the bus. I was never far behind him.

We would go to Browns, which had a big reputation as an exclusive club. You had a main door where you had to knock to gain entry. We got in because we were footballers.

There would be faces you recognised from TV, film, music and sport. Nigel Benn was in the bar used by the players and directors at White Hart Lane once; the cast of *EastEnders* were regulars. We were always surrounded by big names.

I remember we all went to watch the now infamous Watson v Eubank fight at White Hart Lane in September 1991. Watson wore Arsenal shorts and Eubank had the Spurs badge on his. We had been hammered 5-1 by Wimbledon away. We still managed to get smashed on the team bus, even on that short journey across London.

They got passes for us to to go behind the scenes and meet the boxers; obviously Watson was very seriously injured – we did not realise that then – but we saw Eubank in the dressing room after the fight. He was giving Gazza a hard time about looking after himself, and what he ate and drank. Gazza, being Gazza, it went in one ear and out the other.

There is no doubt there is more razzmatazz playing for Spurs in London. It may have had something to do with Terry Venables; he enjoyed showbusiness and loved to mix with actors, singers; 'crooning' at his club, Scribes, was his guilty secret. We saw Adam Faith at a game once because he had written the TV series *Budgie* with the gaffer. In the early days with Gazza on nights out – and even the time after he went back to Lazio – the lads could not believe the celebrities we came across.

One night we met Elton John, George Michael, the singers Pepsi and Shirley, and a woman I did not recognise who turned out to be Petula Clark in Browns. It was quite a night standing next to George Michael and asking him about his latest album with Elton John at the bar. I wish I could remember what we said! Another time, Rod Stewart and his then wife Rachel Hunter were there. When I was at Manchester City, you were more likely to bump into Little And Large.

Even after he left the club, and was living in Italy, Gazza would regularly come back for a night out.

One of my favourite ever Gazza tales came after he had left Spurs for Lazio. When he returned to the UK, he would stay in a hotel near Hyde Park where the manager was a mad keen Spurs fan. He loved Gazza so much, all the Tottenham players got to stay for free.

In one visit home, Gazza took the manager out for the night, got him drunk, somehow found his passport, flew him back to Rome and, en route, shaved off all the fella's hair and eyebrows. He woke up in Gazza's place in Italy not having a clue where he was, or how he had got there. Then he looked in the mirror to discover all his hair and eyebrows had gone as well. When he looked to Paul for an explanation, there came back the usual answer: "It was for a laugh."

•••••••

COCAINE

When I look back now, I took so many risks; I never took drugs in front of the other players. They knew nothing. We would go to late bars, nightclubs, gentlemen's clubs, wine bars – anywhere for a late drink. I would often end up in a club where most of the clientele were on drugs.

In those days, they never bothered with the booze. You walked into the brightly lit loos at 3am and everyone was goggle-eyed, but drinking water. It was strobe lights and Manchester music, bouncing up and down on the dance floor to tunes like *24 Hour Party People*, which was a favourite of mine. And there was I, right in amongst them. It was like hiding in plain sight. If anyone recognised me, they never called the papers. It was the time before camera phones, mobiles, new media. So, somehow, I got away with it, and kept going back for more. As a high profile footballer, an England star as I had become, I knew the stakes were high and yet I still could not stop myself.

On one occasion, I did not want to take cocaine in the loos so I had it in a bag and was using a straw to put it up my nose in a back alley behind a pub.

Unbeknown to me, two plain clothed cops had followed me out and emptied my pockets.

I had the drugs in a bag with the straw in my hand.

"You're Paul Stewart aren't you?" one of the cops said to me.

There was no way I could deny anything.

"Yes," I told him

There was a pause.

All sorts of things flashed through my mind.

National newspaper headlines. Being called into the boss's office and getting the sack. The disgrace. The shame on my family. *This is it*, I thought. *You've pushed it too far.* I had a terrible premonition of the arrest, the handcuffs, being led away to a police station, trying to explain it all to Bev.

Then, after a while, one of the cops just looked at me and said: "On your bike!"

I could not get out of there quick enough. I don't know if they were Spurs fans who had taken pity on me or maybe they just couldn't be bothered with the publicity nicking me would bring. I don't know why they let me off.

When I got home, I thought: *You don't know how lucky you are.*

Looking back now, I think: *Was I really that lucky?*

Could I have sorted myself out if I had been arrested and the problem became public? Could I have gone on to win more caps for England?

I might also have saved myself hundreds of thousands of pounds. Of course, it never did come out – and I will never know.

All former addicts will tell you: you take the first line, and that is it, you are chasing that initial high all the time after that. You have it and think 'one line, one line more', but 100 is never enough. That first line is just a catalyst to do more and more, you are chasing the buzz you get, that feeling first time around. But, of course, you never get it back. With heroin, it is called chasing the dragon. With cocaine, you are just constantly trying to replicate that first kick.

The testers who came to the big clubs in those days tended to go for the younger kids, so I just took the risk. I started to look for the high time and time again. But it was a chicken and egg scenario – every time you went looking, the downers were even worse.

COCAINE

My thoughts about ending it all became more and more frequent, because of the abuse, the legacy of my childhood. Yet here I was, capped by England, in demand, there was no rational reason for the risks, other than the escape from the darkness in my mind.

Back then cocaine was classed as a rich man's drug. It was offered for nothing at times when I was at Spurs. If I was buying it, the cost would be about £50 a gram. It got to the stage where there were people buying it for me. They probably thought they were doing me a favour. In reality, it was the last thing I needed. It was people I socialised with, people I thought I could trust, people I was probably drinking with – what my counsellor later called 'my cocaine friends'.

Within a matter of weeks after trying coke for the first time, it was a regular habit.

In 1992, I think Venables may have heard what I was up to. You could disappear in London to a degree, but it was clear that I was coming into training stinking of booze. Selling me was probably borne out of that – even though it came across in the press that I was homesick and unsettled, which I suppose was true too.

Spurs had already forked out around £5m in the transfer market that summer. Neil Ruddock was recruited from Southampton as a possible skipper in the middle of July and a few days later, I was splashed over the back pages: 'Tel Says £2m Paul Must Go,' read one headline.

My days were numbered. I'd enjoyed the finest days of my career at White Hart Lane but it would soon be over. It was time to leave London behind.

Chapter/15

EXILED

After the early days at Blackpool, I had always worked hard, and trained hard. Once I started to play hard, it became more difficult, if not impossible to give my best; and that hit home during my time at Liverpool. You were not supposed to be on the booze for 48 hours before a game at Spurs. I never quite managed that. By the time Liverpool's new manager Graeme Souness came calling with the offer which Spurs could not refuse, the drugs had become a regular habit.

Whilst I suffered quite a few injuries early on, I simply did not look after myself in the way I should have done to make the move a success. Even the weekend I agreed the deal, the temptation of another bender proved too much.

We were on tour in Scotland when Dougie Livermore, the Spurs assistant manager, said: "The boss wants to see you." Venables told me Liverpool were in for me and had made a bid which was accepted – something I already knew as word had reached me.

As I've said, there was a bit of history with Graeme. Rangers had been in for me before I signed for Spurs way back in 1988; I had been told that he was coming to see me play for City. He did not turn up and then I read in the papers he had gone to see Mark Hateley in Monaco instead. Daft as it sounds, it had left a bit of a bitter taste. But Liverpool was still a great place to be for any footballer. I would have crawled over broken glass to play for them, they were one of the biggest clubs in the world.

Spurs instructed me to fly down to London to meet Souness in an airport hotel and as usual, because I did not have an agent, I did all the negotiations myself.

When I got to Heathrow, I was standing waiting for a taxi when a beautiful blonde haired lady started looking across at me. I knew that I recognised her face, and then I realised it was Souness' girlfriend at the time, Karen Levy, a former *Sale of the Century* hostess who would later become his second wife.

She asked me: "Are you going to meet Graeme?" and I said "yes." She smiled and replied: "So am I." When I got to the hotel where we were meeting, I went straight to the bar because I had a fair bit of time to kill.

It was about an hour and a half to our meeting and by the time Graeme turned up, I had a table full of empty *Holsten Pils* bottles in front of me. Many months later, when I got to Liverpool, he told me: "I have heard you have a reputation as a bit of a drinker." I was thinking: *When you signed me, I had about 10 empty lager bottles on the table. Didn't you notice?*

I turned up with a figure for the new contract in my head and stuck with it. They eventually agreed to pay £10,000 a week with a £100,000 signing-on fee spread over 12 months, though Souness was as tough in negotiations as he had been in the tackle in his playing days.

EXILED

Spurs were making a clear £800,000 profit – which was big money in those days – so as I had not asked for a transfer and they sold me, they agreed to pay up my contract, which amounted to about £200,000 after tax.

Instead of heading straight home to Blackpool afterwards – which is what I should have done – I headed straight into old London town, and straight back on the booze.

A deal like that is a fair reason to celebrate. I was in London on the Saturday and not due in Liverpool till the following Monday. The bar was calling. A few drinks turned into yet another all-night bender in central London, boozing heavily until the early hours, taking 'E' and cocaine.

I remember falling out of a club around Leicester Square as dawn broke, the first light hitting my eyes as I emerged from the darkness of yet another cavernous dance floor. I was staggering through theatreland, the West End, past Covent Garden and ended up walking along past Charing Cross station, right in the heart of London.

It was as quiet as you are ever likely to see it, its taxi ranks empty save for a few pigeons, no one around the entrance to the station or the hotel. It wasn't long after 5am when I saw the only other person out on the street at that hour, a down and out, a tramp who said to me: "Aren't you Paul Stewart?" News of the £2.5m move to Liverpool was already out by then. I recall one of those London billboards, probably for the Sunday papers, proclaiming: 'Stewart set for Liverpool.'

There was a second's hesitation then I thought: *There's no point in denying it.* So I just said to him: "Yes I am mate." Perhaps the newspaper hoarding had made him wonder if it really could be me.

It was a far better story than the transfer. The down and out living on the streets of London. The England footballer, the cup final hero, high on drugs and booze, wandering around at dawn in the midst of a £2.5m transfer to one of the biggest clubs in the world.

Even the tramp must have thought: *He is still out drinking at this hour of the morning.* But beyond that look of astonishment as he recognised my face, he never said another word. I went on my way, but I can still see him there, shaking his head.

It was a sign of things to come at Liverpool, not a great start to the biggest move of my footballing career. I should have known better. But I was becoming so gripped by addiction, there were no lessons learned from all those near misses in the past. The cops finding me in a club with cocaine but letting me go. The PFA dinner when the England coach pulled up as we fell out of a cab. Numerous random drug tests at the Spurs training ground when my name did not come out of the hat. I was pushing my luck. Even I must have known that when I was asked to travel north for the medical. It all went fine until they asked for a urine sample.

In a sudden panic about the drugs in my system, I had to say to the club doctor: "I'm really sorry but I cannot seem to pee."

There was this voice in my head saying they must have been testing for drugs and suddenly it hit home. *I could get caught here. The drugs will show up. What have you done? It will blow the whole move.* It was a rare moment of doubt for me. Not usually one to panic, I could feel the hairs going up on the back of my neck as I thought I was finally going to get caught.

To my astonishment, and relief, the doctor said 'no trouble at all' and just asked me to come back at a later date.

EXILED

There followed two hard days of training back in Blackpool. Out came black bin bags under my training gear to sweat as much out of my system as possible before I returned to Anfield. It was hard graft, but I lost about seven or eight pounds in a couple of days, working like a slave with long runs on the beach, trips to the gym, you name it.

Even 48 hours later, there was still that nagging worry about something showing up. A positive drugs test could mean an all-out ban, and a swift return to Spurs. Terry would not have been too impressed – and nor would Bev, by this time counting on me coming home every day to see her and our young son.

As it turned out, for all the sweat and sleepless nights over those intervening days, there really was no reason to get worked up over it.

When I returned to Anfield, they dipped a couple of sticks into the urine sample. Once the Liverpoool doctor had checked to see if they changed colour, he explained they were looking for diabetes, and testing kidney function. And nothing else. So the move was still on. But it was hardly the dream start.

•••••••

I am not a fan of Souness because of the way he was with me, and many of the other senior stars, some of them legends at the club.

I found him very arrogant, ignorant even, and I did not think he was a very good man-manager. But there is no one but myself to blame for my lack of success at Liverpool. It remains the biggest regret of my footballing career.

After watching the great Liverpool teams in the past, I knew all about their history when I signed for them. But it was a constant, pointless struggle with Souness.

We had a thing called 'weigh-in day' when he used to check the players' weight to make sure they were not over-eating. There were some real characters in the squad; Ian Rush, Steve Nicol, John Barnes, great pros who did not always take too kindly to being treated like schoolboys. Graeme did not seem to get that at times.

When it was clear that Spurs were prepared to let me go in the summer of '92, there was speculation linking me with a return to Manchester City – again. Then came the dream option, with various stories suggesting Manchester United were going to come in at the last minute. That really would have been something, joining the great Class of '92 as they were about to conquer the world. I'd always said Gazza would have struggled under the tight grip of Alex Ferguson's management. But maybe Fergie would have brought me under control.

In the end, Liverpool were clearly very keen as they forked out nearly two and a half million pounds.

At 27, they should have been getting a man at the peak of his powers. An England international with a proven track record; a midfielder with a boundless work rate and an eye for goals. At current prices, the transfer value would be in the region of £19 million. It is safe to say they did not get what they had paid for; I sold them short. I sold myself short.

In those first two years, I was sluggish and injury prone due to my off the pitch antics.

I did not apply myself, which was at odds with how hard I worked at other clubs. My head had gone. I drank a lot and did a lot of drugs so I just wasn't in the right frame of mind. I would often go on the ale straight from training, and would stay out until about 7pm before heading home to Blackpool – where I still lived when I was at Liverpool.

In those days, there was still very much a drinking culture at Liverpool despite the best efforts of Souness to change it. Many of the old pros would be in the drinking gang. I got on really well with Rushie, and the likes of Jan Molby, Ronnie Whelan, Steve Nicol and John Barnes would regularly come out too. We'd often head into the city centre, making a beeline for the Mathew Street area, near where *The Beatles* famously played *The Cavern*, a venue that had long since been demolished; though there were numerous reminders of the Fab Four hanging on the wall of nearby pubs. Alongside Irish-themed bars and traditional pubs, there were now numerous trendy drinking establishments to choose from. We'd hang out at places like *Labinsky's*, a popular cocktail bar.

We had some lively nights, such as the infamous occasion Don Hutchison got in trouble. When he spotted some female students videoing their graduation he dropped his trousers and said: "Zoom in on this!" so the story goes. A year later he did it again. The *News of the World* pictured him on holiday in Ayia Napa, clearly the worse for wear with only a *Budweiser* label protecting his modesty. Two strikes and he was out – that was the end of his Liverpool career. Apparently Roy Evans said: "If Hutchison is flashing his dick again, that's out of order!"

I didn't go out with the players that often at the start. Initially it was maybe once or twice a week. Later on it wasn't every day but it would be a lot more frequent. I wasn't taking drugs when I first went out. I'd been given a scare by the medical and thought that I'd better keep myself clean. It didn't last.

I was soon chasing the coke buzz, nipping off into the loos to satisfy my habit. It was something I did on my own. None of the players knew what I was doing, though I'm sure they must have had some idea later on.

It would vary how much coke I'd take. It might be one or two wraps on some occasions but if I was in the mood I'd go looking for more. Always chasing but never getting that first high.

There was only random drug testing back then and for some reason, once again, I never got tested. Names would be picked out of a hat during training at Melwood and the staff and managers would usher the chosen players in to give a sample. I never got the tap on the shoulder.

When I look back now, I was taking so many risks...even after what I thought was a close call when I signed for Liverpool. I never took drugs in front of anyone, but it was still dangerous, and I could easily have been caught. It was a real, clear and present danger for a high profile footballer; most people know what you are up to when you are using the loos but going in the cubicle all the time. I knew the stakes were high and yet I still could not stop myself. I was addicted.

In my mind, I was able to hide it, or so I thought. I didn't really care by then. For me, it was the release, an escape from my past, and that was what eventually led to me becoming dependent.

I really believe people saw me as unapproachable, arrogant, even ignorant at that time. It is a bitter regret. I would often walk straight past supporters who had waited outside the changing rooms for an autograph, I wouldn't give them a sideways glance.

I often think what a horrible person I was; if I could turn the clock back then I would. *Will you sign this for me please? No problem mate.* It wouldn't have taken much to change. Even when kids were waiting outside, I was reluctant to stop. I had no right to ignore them, as I often did.

I was uncomfortable and uneasy with that side of being a footballer. But there was no excuse, despite my reticence in those kind of situations. Some of the players would say there was no way I was shy. It was just that I felt more comfortable with players. With people around the football club I was fine, but with strangers it was more difficult to handle. Like I say, though, there was simply no excuse.

••••••••

Souness played me as a striker on a few occasions to try and re-ignite my career at Liverpool, but it just did not happen for me, for whatever reason.

I was seen as their second striker to Rushie for a time, after Dean Saunders was sold to Aston Villa in that first season. I managed just one league goal, against Sheffield United on my dream Anfield debut.

I loved the roar of the Kop as it went in, the noise as you lined up in the tunnel with that famous *This is Anfield* sign right in front of you. You could see fear in the eyes of the opposition. Liverpool had been in their pomp in the late '80s, dominating the league, winning trophies. But that debut goal was to be my last for 24 league games. Liverpool spent the remainder of the season struggling in the new Premier League before finishing sixth.

In rare moments of magic for me at Anfield, I scored twice in the European Cup Winners' Cup first round first leg victory over Apollon Limassol in September 1992, one a right foot shot from outside the area in the opening minutes of the game, the second a flying header shortly before half time. We won that one 6-1.

Rushie was the first over to congratulate me after that first goal, and we hit it off during my time at the club. But professionally, it was all downhill from there. In my last two seasons, I did not play a single game for Liverpool, and ended up being loaned out. It was a nightmare. The only consolation was I made some good friends. There were some real characters in the dressing room. There was fun to be had despite the gloom of the situation I found myself in.

Rob Jones, the full-back, was called *Trigger* after the character in *Only Fools and Horses*; Mark Wright was known as *Dot*, because, like Dot Cotton in *EastEnders*, he had a reputation for complaining all the time; Torben Piechnik got *Picnic* for obvious reasons (he became known as Souness' worst ever signing, taking that mantle from me); Michael Thomas was dubbed *Lester* after Lester Piggot as he had a slight lisp, which was not the kindest of nicknames, but I'd heard worse – Paul Allen at Spurs got *Ollie* because everyone said he looked like Stan Laurel from *Laurel and Hardy* while Pat van den Hauwe, as everyone knows, was simply known as *Psycho*.

The Christmas parties at Anfield, usually organised by Jan Molby, were always good fun. I would go dressed as Elvis, as I do for every fancy dress party. As a newcomer you were expected to stand up on a stool in front of all the players and sing a song. My party piece was the old *Disney* song Zip-a-Dee-Doo-Dah but you would only ever get part of the way through your rendition before the rest of the lads would bombard you with drinks or food. Then we would hold an awards ceremony,

It takes two: Celebrating with Gazza at the Den in 1989. We did everything together

Making my point: I had plenty of brushes with authority during my career – the anger I felt inside often got me in trouble. Here, Tony Adams looks on as I confront the referee

Self-destruct: Restraining Gazza during the FA Cup semi-final against Arsenal in 1991

Happy return: (Above) back on home ground, scoring the winner for Tottenham in the FA Cup third round game at former club Blackpool in January 1991.
(Left) Terry Venables told me to keep Roy Keane quiet in the final

Where's FA Cup ears?: I was more nervous about meeting Princess Diana than I was about the final itself

Party time: Winning the FA Cup back then was the pinnacle of any player's career

Special moment: Scoring the equaliser in the 1991 final. I'd been through a lot to get to this stage in my career and I wasn't going to let the opportunity pass me by – despite Gazza's injury

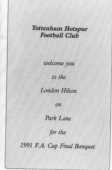

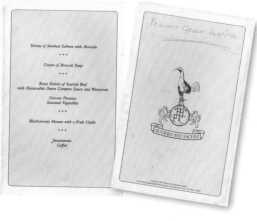

Tottenham Hotspur
Football Club

welcome you

to the

London Hilton

on

Park Lane

for the

1991 F.A. Cup Final Banquet

Terrine of Smoked Salmon with Avocado

* * *

Cream of Broccoli Soup

* * *

Roast Sirloin of Scottish Beef
with Horseradish Onion Compote Sauce and Watercress

Cocotte Potatoes
Seasonal Vegetables

* * *

Blackcurrant Mousse with a Fruit Coulis

* * *

Sweetmeats
Coffee

So proud: (Above) Anthony, Mam and Dad with the silverware. (Left) the post-match banquet card – I scribbled the name of Gazza's hospital on the back!

Two sides: Despite my
England call-up, I was
struggling off the pitch.
I was plagued by thoughts
of my childhood and by
the time I had joined
Liverpool, the drugs had
started to have an impact

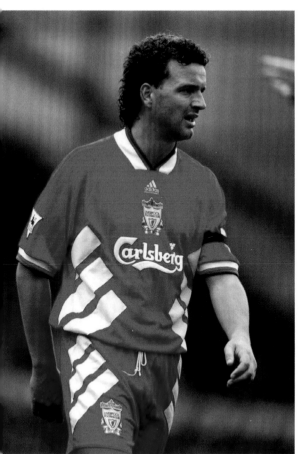

Out in the cold: I was left to rot in the reserves at Liverpool. When the chance came to go out on loan I jumped at it – Crystal Palace (above) being one of the clubs I joined

Second chance: In action for Sunderland in the last match at Roker Park. I would keep playing but it was a relief more than anything else when I finally called time on my career

Turning tide:
The last
year has
seen such a
transformation
in my life

Standing strong:
I owe my family so
much. (From left)
Adam, Bev, Chloe –
with my granddaugher
Sienna – and Jade

one of the prizes being for who had done the most daft things during the season – an award usually claimed by Stevie Nicol.

Stevie was a great bloke and a big character. My favourite Nico story – at least one that can go into print – is when he forgot his suit trousers for an away game against Southampton. For some reason, known only to him, he had replaced his suit 'troosers' with his wife's riding jodhpurs by mistake. When he tried them on in the room, obviously I did not want to give away how funny they looked. I had to pretend they were fine, knowing the reaction he would get from the lads. When he put them on with a suit jacket and tie and went downstairs to the team bus, everybody just fell about laughing.

When I first signed, they were already on tour in Scandinavia and I arrived late to find I was sharing a room with Stevie. All the lads kept asking at dinner: "Is that right you're sharing with Nico?" or "Are you with Bumper?"

They would all smile when I said yes, but not say why. I knew it was a wind-up. He had some interesting habits, and a very unusual way of warming up for games.

Bruce Grobbelaar was another character who had some great stories to tell. His favourite involved 'how to react when faced with an alligator'; he reckoned you could cheat death if you knew what you were doing. There never seemed to be a complete explanation, beyond 'looking into their eyes.'

My son Adam sometimes came with me to training as he grew older, and he loved it at Liverpool, and still supports them to this day.

He remains a big Liverpool fan because he used to kick the ball around with Robbie Fowler, Steve McManaman and Jamie Redknapp when they were still kids at Liverpool. Once we met

Kenny Dalglish and he could not have been nicer with my son; a true legend on the pitch, and off it. Later on, when I went to Sunderland, Adam came into the club there too and was a mascot on one occasion.

••••••••

When Souness clashed with me in front of all the players, I knew the writing was on the wall. It was around 1993, about a year into my time at the club, and it was already becoming clear that I was not in his plans.

Liverpool had been struggling; it was a difficult time at the club. Speculation was rife that Souness was about to leave, and there was a newspaper story which referred to the time left on his contract. I was on the training pitch with all the first team squad. I was never slow to speak my mind, and I was being particularly petulant.

After two laps of the Melwood training ground, he stopped the warm-up, swore and suggested that if I wanted to leave the club, I should ask for a transfer and give up any settlement on the remaining time on my contract. I asked: "Are you going to do the same?" It didn't mean anything, it was just a split second remark borne out of sheer frustration. But I knew there would be consequences from speaking to the boss like that.

If you cannot get into the first team squad, you cannot describe the dejection you feel. Even if I had a brilliant game in the second string, I knew that I was never going to break through.

There was no coaching for me. There were some brilliant young players coming through, the so-called 'Spice Boys' – lads

EXILED

like Robbie Fowler, Don Hutchison, Steve McManaman and, of course, Jamie Redknapp.

The coaches knew they had a big future and so they would be talking to them and working on their game all the time. With me, they just used to throw me a shirt.

It was a situation where they had paid big money for me so they had to put me in the reserves, in the shop window if you like, in case somebody did come in for me. With the salary I was on, they had to give me a game, but I hated every minute of it.

I know that I did appear arrogant at times. Jamie Carragher, in his autobiography, remembers me asking him: "What the fuck are you doing here?" when he turned up to play with us in the reserves. I just cannot recall saying that, but there is every chance I will have done because I was so unhappy.

I actually had a good rapport with many of the young lads. Robbie Fowler was brilliant after I went public about the abuse and gave me a lot of support. He sent a message on Twitter and dedicated a newspaper column to saying how much he admired what I had done. I thanked him because it meant a lot to me, especially after what I had been through at Liverpool, and how difficult I was there at times.

What made the problem worse was the fact that Liverpool never received a concrete offer for me. Manchester City came in and wanted to sign me because Peter Reid was there with Sam Ellis at the time and they were keen to get me back to Maine Road. I would have loved that, but the history with Peter Swales during my time there meant he put a block on it. He told Reidy, "I'm not having him here again," and, of course, he signed the cheques, so that was the end of that.

It did not get much better once Souness went. Roy Evans,

195

who took over as manager, never gave me a look-in. It was pure misery.

I played for the reserves at Southport on a regular basis, and there would be a crowd of 500 shouting all kinds of abuse. *You're shite Stewart. No wonder you didn't make it. What a waste of money.* I was not exactly Mr Popular and, unlike in the big games at Anfield with the buzz from the stands, you could hear every word of criticism at Haig Avenue.

It was the lowest point of my football career being at Liverpool. There was never any light at the end of the tunnel. It's a lonely feeling being left out in the cold, no matter what your profession. I grew to hate having to drive down to training every day. It was a job I despised.

The only release I knew from it all was going out, drinking and taking more drugs. It was a vicious spiral. I came off the coke and I was more depressed than ever.

When the chance came to get sent out on loan, I grabbed it. I ended up going to a few teams while I was at Liverpool: Crystal Palace, Wolves, Burnley and Sunderland. At the very least I was training with the first teams again, and in or around the first eleven for games.

At Palace, I met Gareth Southgate for the first time. It was 1994; I played 18 games, scored three goals, and we won the old second division together at Palace. I got a loan move there through Steve Harrison, who I knew through the England set-up.

He suggested they get me on loan to play with Chris Armstrong up front. So I went with him down there and you could see from day one that Southgate was a manager for the future. Never for one moment did I think then he would be in charge of England one day. But the way he conducted himself was admirable; and I am pleased for him. It is such a tough job now, we are slipping down the world rankings, you wonder if they should start to regulate the number of overseas players in the teams, we never seem to get the chance to play England prospects due to players from abroad. Without radical change, without nurturing young talent like Fergie's Class of '92, then we have no chance.

It was good of Southgate, in his first days as England boss after Sam Allardyce's shock departure, to mention me in his statement on the abuse scandal. He referred to 'one of his old team-mates coming forward.' It was a great message of support.

Old friends in the game tried to help me out even in my darkest times at Anfield, but it didn't always go according to plan. I had a rough time on loan at Burnley, getting sent off in my first two games. I got so much stick from their fans, I gestured to take my shirt off and throw it in the crowd.

About six months later, manager Jimmy Mullen had got the sack and former Everton star Adrian Heath, who took over, rang me. He said: "Do you fancy coming back to Burnley?" I said: "If I was you, I would speak to someone first." The local paper did the story that the club was after me and they were inundated with complaints from fans saying they were going to burn their season tickets!

Inchy, as we called him, then rang me and said: "What did you do when you were up here? You were only here for a couple of weeks."

We decided it would not be a good idea to go back.

Despite my drug issues, I was still a very strong character in the dressing room, no matter where I went, and if players did have a go at me, I would either get my revenge on the training pitch, by getting stuck in, or verbally. Back then, I got even with team-mates, and I did not mind how.

The natural law of the dressing room dictated that you had to stand up for yourself and my survival instincts had been well honed from my teenage experiences. With the Spurs lads, there was great dressing room banter and, though it was mainly in good spirit, any slight sign of weakness and God help you. It was the same at Liverpool.

Come the 1995/96 season, when Peter Reid came in for me and asked me to sign for Sunderland, I could not wait to get away from Anfield. There had been so many downs on the drink and drugs, I also knew it was the last chance for me.

I had to get clean, to get fit, and to stop taking the drugs.

Chapter/16

COLD TURKEY

In the summer of 1996, I knew that I had a serious habit. I had to stop taking cocaine – and ecstasy, which I still used.

The only problem was, I had to do it myself, without telling anyone, including Bev. I was still very much leading a double life and as far as I was concerned, my addiction was a secret that even my wife knew nothing about.

Getting off the drugs involved going 'cold turkey' for the best part of two weeks. I told Bev that I would sleep alone because I wasn't feeling too well. I didn't go into details, just set myself up in the spare room of our Blackpool home, and took it from there. It is hard to describe the nightmares, hallucinations and physical extremes which coming off cocaine entails. I was taking coke on a regular, if not daily basis, so I knew that getting clean would not be easy.

I would go to bed and have dreams which were a mixture of unconscious thoughts and real life; bright colours, a weird array of visions. I would experience something completely random and obscure when I was asleep, but I'd be convinced that I was awake. When I was awake, the opposite would happen; I would think I was sleeping. My mind was being pulled in different directions.

My body was suffering too. I felt hot, but I kicked off the blankets and my skin was cold; it was just ridiculous. I started to realise just how serious my problem had been.

And I was going through all of this without telling a soul, because it was a secret, even from my close family.

I had very little sleep for about 10 days. It did not take a full two weeks to come off the coke, but that withdrawal, the visions and confusion was a constant. I would get up choking for a drink and down a pint of water. I'd pick up a bit but then just feel terrible again once I lay my head down.

Despite everything, I wasn't scared.

I was determined to carry on because I was in such a bad place. I knew I had to get through it – there was no alternative. After four years of being written off, of going through the hell of Liverpool reserves and being thrown on the scrapheap, I knew that if I was ever to revive my career as a footballer, then I had to tough it out.

I just said to myself: *I don't care if this takes another five days... or it kills me. It can't get any worse.* I couldn't get any lower. I thought: *I have to accept the consequences of what I have done, the addiction is down to me. If I die, so be it...*

So while the rest of the country was enjoying Gazza and Shearer at Euro 96, I wasn't sure when my cold turkey was going to end. But I got through it. The dreams and hallucinations stopped. I no longer saw monsters in the night. By the time the 1996/97 Premier League season started, believe it or not, I was close to peak condition.

COLD TURKEY

I replaced the drink and drugs with a proper fitness regime in the De Vere Hotel gym near my home, where I was working out for three hours a day.

That was supplemented by a proper diet, eating all the right things, giving up the booze. Reidy knew it as soon as I arrived for my first pre-season; more importantly, so did I. I was not selling anyone short. Funnily enough, you can see it on the photos from that period of my career.

It sounds strange to say it after playing for England and scoring in a FA Cup final. But staying clean at Sunderland, at Stoke City, even at Workington – I see that as as one of the real achievements of my career.

I had to keep saying to myself: *I've got to stay off the drugs*. Achieving that was like winning a cup final. I say that because of the level of my addiction. During the dark days,I had been spending around £300 to £500 a week on drugs.

After getting clean, it was about proving myself on the pitch and going on to become a regular. At Sunderland, and subsequently at Stoke City, I was in the team week in, week out – and that felt really good. Fit again, and playing at the very top.

I first joined up with Reidy in March '96, around the time my third child and second daughter, Jade, was born. She came into the world on March 17, the same day we were playing Birmingham City in a televised game. Reidy broke the news to me at the pre-match meal, shouting over: "Stewy, it's a girl!"

Sunderland were riding high in Division One when I arrived. The people were great and the passion of fans was obvious from the off.

I am one of very few players to appear in a north London derby, a Manchester derby, a Merseyside derby and a North

East derby. If you ever get this question in a pub quiz – or on one of those machines: 'Who played in all the major derbies between teams in the Premier League?' – the answer is Paul Stewart. But they do cheat a bit. The Manchester derby was a testimonial game, for Jimmy Nichol.

All those derbies meant that I understood the importance of the games against Newcastle for Sunderland fans; at Spurs, we always knew we had to perform against Arsenal; Everton were intense rivals when I was at Liverpool. Score in that game and you become a hero overnight. You enter into folklore.

Reidy took me under his wing. He understood how important it was for me to prove myself. And he used that desire as a tool to get the best out of me. In the 1995/96 season, it really worked. I was playing in a squad alongside the likes of Michael Gray, Kevin Ball, Gary Bennett and Paul Bracewell, talented players who knew the area. We kept on winning and Reidy took us to the First Division title.

I knew I had to get myself totally straight that summer if I was to prove myself again in the Premiership.

When I arrived back in the North East in July, I remember Bobby Saxton, Reidy's number two – *Sacko* as we called him – knocking me on the head and saying: "Is everything right up there?" It was clear what he meant.

Did I have my head straight? More importantly, was I off the drugs? Reidy was such a shrewd operator, he would have heard some of the rumours going around at Liverpool and would have known about my lifestyle. He was giving me a second chance – and I was determined not to blow it.

•••••••

COLD TURKEY

It became clear at some stage that season that we did not have a side with the ammunition to survive in the Premiership. In the good times, I had been staying at the Royal County in Durham, and Reidy would say to me on a Saturday night 'see you Thursday.' He knew he could trust me and that I wouldn't let him down. My head was clear and I was determined to keep it that way.

Reidy also knew that I would come back and be training in Blackpool by myself. Steve Black, then a Gateshead Harriers fitness coach who went on to work for Newcastle United and Jonny Wilkinson, gave me a three hour programme.

It was a very tough work-out. I would be thinking: *I've got to go through this again.* There were stretches, weights, anaerobic work, a series of general fitness exercises, a warm-down. I did that every day without fail. I really looked after myself. I was in good shape.

Once we got to the Premiership, and started to lose, naturally the ethic and regime changed. All of a sudden, it would be: 'In on a Monday.' Then, when things got really bad, it was: 'In on Sunday.'

To be honest, we were unlucky, and did not have a bad start. Reidy had brought in some big personalities, big names, and they made a difference, even at that level.

Niall Quinn cost £1.3m, and from his very first season, you could see he was going to become a firm favourite with the fans. My old mate Tony Coton came from Manchester City and was a big influence too. Chris Waddle, in the twilight of an outstanding career, came in for his swansong and could still beat a man with the deft drop of a shoulder or a shuffle of those lightning feet.

The new 42,000-seater Stadium of Light was due to be ready by the summer of 1997, so that debut season in the Premiership, there was a feeling of a club going places. I scored against Villa in October to grab three vital points and by mid-season, we looked comfortable in 11th position in the league.

But we hit trouble and straight defeats against Villa, Leeds United, Blackburn Rovers and Tottenham saw us slip at a crunch time in the season. We had beaten Chelsea (3-0), Arsenal (1-0) and Manchester United (2-1) all at home, but lost out in the final match of the campaign.

For me, there was only one shining light. If Paul Gascoigne was the best player I ever played with, Eric Cantona was the best I ever played against. I was in the side that lost 5-0 to Man United at Old Trafford just before Christmas in '96. Cantona was so arrogant it was untrue, but he had the ability to back it; he toyed with us that day. He scored the now famous goal, said to be his best ever, when he chipped it over the Sunderland goalkeeper Lionel Perez and into the top corner, then turned and puffed his chest out.

I remember Reidy had instructed our centre half Kevin Ball, who was hard as nails, to follow his every move. If he could do that, he told him, then we'd have a chance. I think he was being a bit optimistic; Bally never got anywhere near him. If he went to kick him in the air, Cantona knew and would just lay it off really simple first time. If he backed off and gave him a bit of space he would do something magic with it. It was like watching a conductor with his orchestra and – don't tell Reidy this – it was a privilege to be on the same pitch as him.

I went up to Cantona after the game to shake hands and, of course, there was no acknowledgment and he just completely ignored me. I probably gave him a few choice words, something derogatory but there was no response whatsoever. He may not have seen me, but you tend to expect that kind of thing where there has been some kind of needle – not when nothing has happened between you.

I remember the story about the United team all going to a film premiere and they were told to wear black ties. Eric turned up in a cream lemon suit and Nike trainers. Ferguson apparently told him he looked fantastic. That's what happens when you are touched by genius, I suppose.

One of the reasons I did not go into management was that I always thought a big part of it was how to get the best out of individuals, and Fergie sums that up for me. At that stage of my career, making me perform did not mean training all the time, even if we were losing.

Many fans see management as tactical training more than anything but in reality man-management was one of the most important aspects for me during my career. I am a bit fiery at times, even now. Even running my own business, I will shoot from the hip and tell people what I think straight away.

That is how you end up at employment tribunals as a boss. You have to be much more considered. Honesty is hard in football because of the pressures. There are managers telling you 'of course you are still part of my plans.' Once you close the office door, they are on the phone trying to sell you or set up a swap deal.

That was hard for me to take, even in the twilight of my career. I know people will say: 'How can you talk that way and still do drugs?' I was not using them to enhance my performance on the pitch, quite the contrary; it was part of my make-up, the way I dealt with the past. But I like people to be straight. I am very black and white in working with people, and I find it hard to see the grey areas sometimes.

After Sunderland's relegation, I found myself at Stoke City. The '97/'98 season was a difficult one for the club and there was some unrest among the squad. Goalkeeping legend Neville Southall was there after leaving Everton and supported by Kevin Keen, the midfielder, he came up with the idea of going to see the board to state the players' case. As the senior pro, I was made the shop steward – the spokesman, if you like – and made my way up to see the directors. This was all agreed with the younger players beforehand

"Look," I told the board, "the players are not happy with the management team you have brought in."

The directors listened and then decided to ask the players for themselves. "Who is not happy about this?" they asked the squad when they were all together.

Only Neville spoke up for me. The rest just kept their heads down. Next thing you know, I'm out of the Stoke team.

In the last match of the season, Stoke played my old club Manchester City and if either team won they could have stayed up in the old second division, depending on other results. City won 5-2 but both teams were relegated to the third tier of English football, a dark day for both sets of supporters.

Despite that and everything that had happened, Stoke wanted me to stay on and join the coaching team. But I'd had enough of going back and forth to Staffordshire from Blackpool. It was an hour and a half drive and I spent so much time on the road, I even started to learn Spanish with one of those language tapes on the three-hour drive to and from training.

COLD TURKEY

I decided to go to Workington for the twilight years of my career. It was closer to home and it meant I would see the kids every day. Some people were shocked by the move. It was a big drop down yet, for a short time at least, I rediscovered my passion for the game.

••••••••

I turned pro in October 1981 when I had just turned 17. It's funny when you see the photos of me back then, still spotty and looking every inch the wide-eyed kid, straight out of school.

I was in at the deep end; four months later, up against seasoned pros who liked to test the newcomer on the block, stick a foot in, try you out with a careful dig in the ribs when the ref wasn't looking. I may have been a teenager, and green as grass despite my situation, but I was a big lad even then, and I learned to give as good as I got.

I can remember my first match like it was yesterday; going through everything in my mind both before and after the game, feeling like my big moment had arrived at last.

The last match in my career came more than 18 years later for Workington Town in the Northern League Premier first division. The Christchurch Meadow ground may not sound like much of a farewell but by the time I stepped out there, I knew it was the end of the road.

According to the official stats, it was my 600th game, not a bad run given some of the incredible ups and downs along the way.

It was a strange feeling as I came off for the last time – we had won but finished mid-table, as did our opponents Belper, so it was a classic end of season encounter with nothing riding on it; for me, there was no emotion, and no regrets.

I went to Workington because many of the fixtures were in and around the North West. The family was well settled in Blackpool by then. The kids were either sorted at school, or starting to make their way in the world.

Bev was happy in our home – we had bought a nice house with a big garden, frequently used for summer barbecues – and we regularly had family and friends around.

I was surprised by how much the move to Workington re-ignited my love for the game.

After a rollercoaster of a career which lasted almost two decades, learning my trade at Blackpool, banging them in for City, the glitz and glamour of life in London with Gazza and Spurs, and the grim despair of being on the sidelines for years at Liverpool, I would turn up for matches to find lads who had just done 12 hour night shifts and were still raring to go, doing it for the sheer love of the game. It felt great to be part of it.

It made me realise what a privileged position I had been in as a pro. There were memories of training on a Monday during my professional career when some of the lads would be complaining about turning in two days after a match. At times I would be among the ones moaning.

Playing semi-pro, I began to realise, for the first time, just how lucky I had been. I would find myself at places like Trafford, Gretna, Chorley, Matlock Town, Lincoln Utd and Whitley Bay, and of course there were times when I would look back and think of the glory days.

We won the title – albeit the North West Counties League – in my first season, to go up into the Northern Premier League first division, and it was what I needed at that time. Of course, I knew that I was coming to the end of my career but I wanted to keep on playing as long as I could.

I often travelled to games with Blackpool legend Jimmy Armfield's son John – who I still see at my local golf club, and Derek Mountfield, the former Everton centre half, who would bring his trophies and medals in when the lads asked him.

I was on £500-a-game and when it came to the end of the second season I went to see them and explained I was about to retire. I did not feel right taking the money. I was 35 and my body could no longer do what my mind was telling it to.

There was a realisation that it was all over which I find hard to explain now, just an instinct as much as anything; I knew the time was right. In truth, I had known for a while. My head was writing cheques that my body could not cash. Every centre half wanted to make a mark in games against me because I had been an England player.

I did not want to risk life and limb at that stage of my career, and at the same time, I wanted to be fair to the team.

Workington offered me the role of player-manager when I told them I was quitting, but I left with every intention of retiring from work for good, just playing golf.

Little more than six months later, I realised there was no way that was going to happen – I was too young, and needed to find something else to do. Going without the buzz of football left too big a void in my life.

Trouble and temptation were lying in wait for me.

Chapter/17

TURNING RIGHT

October, 2000

I have just turned 36.

I am in the Jacuzzi in the De Vere Hotel, Blackpool, and the first day of the rest of my life – the early retirement which I had been looking forward to for so long – happened just six months ago.

As I look around, a realisation suddenly dawns on me, one which has not really struck me before: *You are the youngest here by about 30 years Paul. What are you doing? And what are you going to do with the rest of your life?*

The gym trips are an effort to try and look after myself, keep fit and make use of the hours when the kids are at school during the day; but I have fallen into some bad habits, partly due to the time on my hands.

A few months after I've finished playing, I find myself in a pub in Blackpool. After I have had a few pints, I am offered cocaine by an acquaintance. I weigh it up in my head. *Well, it's only one line. It can't hurt. It's no big thing. It's not like I have to get up in the morning.*

I had been clean for the best part of six years and was very proud of that achievement.

In my mind, that first time, I wasn't doing anything wrong. You tell yourself: *I won't let it get to me. I can handle it.* Of course, you never can.

Before you know it, you become addicted again.

Poulton-le-Fylde, near Blackpool, had already become a regular hang-out for a drink. There is a photo of me, aged around 18, in a bar called The Old Town Hall. It's a traditional ale house with a good crowd of regulars. Great atmosphere, pool table, juke box, decent beers.

I was shopping one day, not long after my last game, and nipped in for a pint. I met some friends from way back when, people I knew from my playing days and they invited me to meet them for a night out. That became a routine.

There were a number of boozers all within a two or three minute walk of each other. We would often meet at The Old Town Hall, before walking around the corner to the Thatched House or the Golden Ball.

They are all close to the pedestrianised zone which is full of eager shoppers on market days. I have some good friends working on the stalls there and I see them now to play golf and have a 'regular' drink without the drugs.

But back then, I would often end up in a late bar called The Cube, which sits on the corner of the main thoroughfare and right opposite The Thatched House. You could get a drink there until 2am, but really it was just an excuse to stay up late when I was flying on drugs. When the bar shut, it did not end there. There would be another 'one for the road' at someone's house nearby and, before you knew it, you would be heading for home at four or five in the morning for a few hours' kip before heading into work.

It became a regular drink and drugs crawl. Drink. Drugs. Drink. Drugs. Drink. Drugs. Sleep. Work. And Repeat. Despite the needs of my business, I used to find a way to keep it all going.

That daily cycle lasted ten years of my life.

I became well and truly addicted for the simple reason that I wasn't ready to face up to my life; to confront the reason why I was lonely and empty. I was in denial and taking drugs every day was the perfect way to block out the real world.

•••••••

It was 2010 when I found myself in a clinic for addicts close to my home. I should have visited long before then.

It was Bev who told me that I had to get help. And I could sense that she meant 'get help, or this time it really is the end of our marriage.'

By then, the never-ending drink and drug binges had taken their toll. I was 45 years old. The kids were now getting older. Adam was about to start out on a life on his own, working for me in Australia, making his way in the world. But I was still stuck in my old ways.

When I found a clinic in Blackpool, it was not the escape I had expected.

At first I had tried the Professional Footballers' Assocation. Though they were very good more recently, when I went public over the abuse, back then I was a voice in the wilderness. There were messages left, asking for help:

> *This is Paul Stewart, former footballer. I need your help. I have issues with drugs that I am struggling to resolve. My marriage is in trouble...*

No response. Instead, I headed to the drugs advisory service which is located off Blackpool seafront. There were no famous people at the door queuing up for counselling. This was not Betty Ford in Hollywood.

There was no Tony Adams, Paul Merson, or Paul Gascoigne waiting to see me before I walked into the world of *Sporting Chance*, and those people who had dealt with Premier League stars – the ones who had seen all the big names, pop stars, celebrities, footballers, down the years.

This was an end of terrace, pebble-dash-fronted property which could have passed for an old people's home. Right in the middle of the run-down streets now full of B&Bs for people on the housing list.

Inside, I found myself in a waiting room with heroin addicts, desperate for their methadone replacement therapy.

As I sat there, looking into the haunted faces of people whose lives have been wrecked and written off, the desperate and addicted who will beg, steal and borrow for their next fix, I thought: *Don't think you are any better than them, because you are just the same, Paul. This is what drugs have done to you. This is how you end up.*

TURNING RIGHT

Despite the flash car parked outside and the England caps and awards pinned up on the office wall, I had been reduced to this. I quickly learned that drugs has no respect for the rich and famous because you always end up in the same place. There was not much fun to be had for all the amusement arcades, the trams and the tower just around the corner. Instead, I was sitting inside a tiny waiting room with what many would say were the 'down and outs', looking at the pamphlets and posters of a needle exchange.

Those early sessions were the hardest. The counsellor was ideal because he was a former addict. He listened intently to what I had to say, but did not judge in any way.

Yet he told me the cold, hard truth.

The only person who could get me out of this mess was right there in the room.

And that person was me.

He said: "You have your coke friends that you take drugs with, and your real friends. You had better find your real friends now."

For those first few weeks, I honestly thought that I would never get by. I feared there would be no one there to meet me for a friendly drink at the end of a working day.

But deep down, I knew he was right.

There came a time when I finished work where I could go left. To meet the coke friends. Or I could turn right, to see the lads who I had known for years who never went down the drug route, those people who were quite happy to see me for a pint and a catch-up.

It sounds simple, and I guess for some it would be, but it took mental focus to keep my mind on recovery.

Going cold turkey again was far from simple.

This time, it wasn't a secret. Bev knew why I was ill; she knew what I was going through.

I locked myself in the bedroom when I thought I needed coke, and did not go out. There were the same hot and cold sweats I had experienced when I first de-toxed. Coke may not be heroin, it is not as bad as other drugs. But obviously I had been on it for 10 years. Five hundred pounds a week buys you a lot of coke in Blackpool.

Coming off it the first time, after I left Liverpool, was easier because I hadn't used it so frequently and over such a prolonged period. And I was also still young, and fit.

My motivation back then was the need to save my career, a pride in doing right by Reidy, the man who had put his trust in me when many others wondered why. By the age of 45, I was truly in deep.

It was mind over matter. I have never relied on medication to get me off drugs, it was just sheer guts that saw me through and once again, the cold sweats gradually lessened.

I won't pretend that I could forget the past because that would be a lie. The memories were still there and they came into my head so often that I just had to deal with them as best I could. Sometimes that would mean an early night.

The drugs counsellor, a complete stranger, listened intently as I spoke about the impact of the abuse. He patiently guided me as to the best way forward. The abuse was not the major concern back then. It had caused the addiction, and that is what I needed to really address. So it was a case of 'let's get off the drugs first, and see what we can do.'

At first, I would be seeing him a couple of times a week, then maybe once depending on how I felt. I could still call him after those initial 12 months of counselling. I felt that he understood me straight away; in fact, it was like he knew me inside out. That felt good. Perhaps if I had not had such a strong bond with my counsellor, I might have found it more difficult.

The first session with Bev was probably the toughest of all. My head wasn't clear from drugs. It was only the Monday after another heavy weekend.

As I sat there, my wife beside me, I just said to myself: *I have to try.* So I started telling my story. Suddenly, Bev was exposed to my drugs secrets in all their horrific detail. The money I had wasted on coke, the mad all-night sessions before getting up and going off to work, the bleak, dark periods of coming down. At least it meant she understood the past.

Once abused, you are fearful of putting trust into somebody because they may let you down again. That was at the heart of the early problems in my marriage; it has defined my entire adult life in terms of relationships. They talk about paedophile coaches making the ultimate abuse of trust, and I have lived through that. It is hard to open up to anyone afterwards; the most innocuous comment becomes a personal attack.

The drugs meant everyone was my friend – for a little while – and I could forget the past, escape the anger which I carried all the time, right throughout my playing career.

It may have been the counselling, or simply age, the passing of time, but I have lost that anger now.

That is the difference between me, and some of the people who I have met as a result of the scandal; their anger is still fresh, it is still there. I feel like I have have moved on. I hope they can somehow find the same escape.

Some nights, sleep can still be elusive. It may be that I just get four hours, but that is more than I had before, and even up at dawn, I can function at work and for the rest of the day.

With drugs, you have to hit rock bottom before you realise you need help – for me, that process took ten long years. My counsellor confirmed what I thought – that I was well and truly addicted in that period, that decade after I finished football. I desperately needed to change.

The counselling helped me to understand the reasons for my addiction, how to address them and how to end the cycle of taking coke to control how I felt.

So many people who develop a habit end up in jail. At least I have survived it all without it totally ruining my life. Being a survivor, if I can call it that, I suppose is a testament to my character.

••••••••

Being clean enabled me to go back to work and turn my attention to the business, which despite everything was thriving. I started to look at building a customer base in Australia, Canada, and beyond.

We were also selling our electronic advertising as an idea in football grounds back then. Though the clubs gradually started to do their own thing, it was a very profitable side of the business at first. I'd spotted a gap in the market and I knew I had a talent for business; something that would give me a new purpose and ambition in life.

And, of course, I 're-discovered' my family. I would usually be out all the time, so now it was nice just to relax with them in the house; watching television, having breakfast, doing the simple things without feeling like I should be somewhere else. Previously, if I was out for an early Sunday lunch with the family, I would be distracted, counting down the minutes until I was meeting my mates and starting the drink and drugs cycle all over again. Quite often it was Chloe who dropped me off at the pub.

Now, my brother and sister-in-law would come around and we would spend time in the garden if the weather was nice. On one occasion, we went to a show in Manchester, to see *The Rat Pack – Live From Las Vegas*. They didn't know it, but I was sitting there in the audience with a tear in my eye; it just felt so good to be enjoying it naturally, experiencing all the emotions as I was meant to. It felt special.

I am not complacent. You never know what is around the corner and I am always aware of that. With addiction, you have to be mindful of the dangers because they are always there. If you think you have beaten addiction, it can come back into your life all over again. Even now, when I am out, there are people offering me drugs all the time.

If they have not seen me for a while, they assume you are still using. They'll spot you in a bar and sidle up to you, ask you if you want some. I just shake my head and tell them: "I'm not on it anymore, mate." My life lesson is: *never take the dangers for granted*. I don't want to go back to the dark days. I know now that for all the 'ups', there are far more downs.

During my darkest days on coke, I would be lying in bed and feel my heart pounding in my chest. It felt so loud, I would become convinced that Bev, lying by my side, might hear it. Sometimes I had to get up and leave the bedroom.

I survived those short term horrors of coming off drugs but there are longer term physical consequences I now have to deal with.

In March 2016, when I was on holiday in Spain, I experienced a heart flutter. I also noticed that I was out of breath, just walking uphill. As soon as we got back, Bev got me in for checks and I had to have various scans and an ECG test.

Initially, it was diagnosed as an irregular heartbeat called atrial fibrillation, also known as AF. That is a condition that can lead to blood clots, stroke, heart failure and complications.

They would be concerned about AF if you are 70, but at 51 it is young to have that kind of problem with your heart and they were not happy just leaving it, so in February 2017, I went in for an operation to sort it out. I didn't want to worry the kids, so I played it down a fair bit, especially as Chloe was pregnant.

I was under a general anaesthetic for just short of five hours. The recovery has been fine. I had to go back, in case I needed a pacemaker fitted but they said the operation had been a success and it wasn't needed.

I am convinced the heart condition and operation are the aftermath of the drugs. It makes me think that I wish I had gone to counselling earlier than I did, recognised why I was taking coke and learned how to stop the cycle. But it could be worse. I'm grateful I've survived.

In 2010, I had come to a turning point. I knew that I had to get the monkey off my back, the need to take coke on a daily basis. I did not feel like I needed it when I woke up in the morning – it was not like that for me, not like an alcoholic craving his first vodka with his cornflakes.

Yet it was like having a pint in the evening – taking cocaine became a regular occurrence. And my counsellor told me: "It might get you at some point."

If I am offered drugs now, the important thing is to feel no embarrassment when you are saying no; to not react badly when they ask. They are thinking of the man they met before. Paul Stewart, *the coke head*.

That person is gone now, I have had to banish him forever. But you know that you can never take anything for granted.

You have to keep on saying 'no' and turning right.

Chapter/18

BEV'S STORY

Tough love

I had known even before our wedding day 29 years ago that there was a secret in Paul's past. His mum had told me that he did not speak for a year as a child. When I heard that, I knew that just could not be right. That something bad must have happened to him, to cause that terrible reaction.

Paul was always very deep; you could never tell what he was thinking. He had me wondering from one moment to the next what mood he would be in. From early on in our relationship, even during those early days in Blackpool together, buying our first home, then having Adam – before we had married – he was hard to work out. But it was not until he went public that I fully understood why.

I thought going public as Paul did was a tremendously brave thing to do and we were behind him 100 per cent. I did not know the truth until he told the full story, and by then we had been married for a long time. Paul was in digs with a lady called Pat very early in his career in Blackpool.

I had only just met Paul but Pat and I really hit it off, we got on so well right from our first meeting. One night I went around for a glass of wine and we got talking, as women do, about relationships, kids, plans for the future. That year of silence came up and Pat's reaction was just the same as mine. "That's not right, is it? Something must have gone on."

Both of us knew something sinister must have happened – a young child not uttering a word for a year. We just knew that something was buried there in his past. We could never have guessed just how bad it really was. There was no clue until after the wedding.

Paul was in digs in Blackpool with an elderly couple when he first came to the club, and they absolutely adored Frank Roper, I still don't know why. For some reason, Roper was everything to them, and they kept asking why Paul was not inviting Frank to our wedding.

Paul did not want him there and they could not work out why. I found it impossible to explain, and so there was a nagging doubt there about the real reason. They were known as 'Mr and Mrs T' to all the players – they were called Thompson, Alan and Betty – and obviously no one knew then what Frank Roper was really like so they could not get their heads around it. But Paul made sure he was nowhere near.

I had met Roper on a few occasions, in and around Blackpool when Paul was first at the club; but we never had a conversation as he was never in our company. I remember that Paul had to get sportswear from him at times, when he first joined the club, and I went with him to get it. Only now can I really understand how hard that must have been for him, and how horrendous it was, having Roper at the club all the time Paul was there.

I thought back then that he had helped Paul and his family, with his football training when he was growing up, and then with supplying his gear later on at the club.

Roper was there with a gang from Blackpool. He was always in or around the club – and always with the kids, or the young players. It was only when Paul told me later that he had been sexually abused that I fully understood what he was up to; it was a terrible feeling.

●●●●●●●●

We had our big day at Blackpool Registry Office. It is funny seeing the photos now, laughing and joking with my sister Karen. Paul was determined nothing would get in the way of my big day.

The TV cameras turned up, but he had not said a word about his meeting with Terry Venables, about the transfer to Spurs. He became one of the most expensive players ever, right after the wedding. But when we turned up on the telly, on *Granada Reports*, it was just the story of our wedding, with all the family there with us.

After the ceremony and reception were all over, Paul blurted out about some problems with Frank growing up; he was not specific but I knew that it was bad because he was so upset, and I was shocked it was Frank. Paul did not go into any kind of detail when he first told me, and I did not push it. At the time, I did not know how to respond to it, to be honest, so I did not pursue it further.

Over the years, sometimes when he had been drinking, he would talk about it, and that was typical of Paul. He would have a drink to open up, more than anyone I know; but he never said anything when he was sober.

It was a secret, like his use of drugs. A couple of people said he did cocaine, but because they tested in football I just thought he would be found out if he was taking it. That would be risking everything.

I know now what I did not know for many years – he had a secret life, for years and years of our marriage. I did not find out about the drugs until after he stopped playing.

Perhaps I just chose not to believe it, preferred not to face up to that possibility. I knew that he hung out with people who took drugs. But I was so busy looking after the kids, the home, while he was away.

Family life has always been the most important thing for me. There is so much said about footballers' wives. I am not typical by any means; I just do not see myself like that. Football does not float my boat; I rarely went to a match, and never went to a team Christmas 'do'. Back in the day, they tended to do lads' parties for the players. To be honest, and I don't mean this in a negative way, but that suited me just fine.

Even the Saturday games worked for me. There were times during his career, in the tough times of our marriage, when I was thinking: *Thank God he has gone, is he going to be speaking today when he comes back?*

It was very hard for him when he was not playing at Liverpool, and as he came to the end of his career. He would bring all that frustration home with him. People think of footballers and think of the money, that whole life, the glamour if you like. But it is not a guarantee of happiness.

There were things which were just a given. He had to give

so much to his career, and I had to accept that. He missed the births of two of our kids, because of that commitment to work, but I would never question that; it was just work, it was what he had to do.

We are complete opposites, that is absolutely true and many people comment on it, and ask how we have lasted so long. We are so different, but he is funny, he makes me laugh, we have good nights out, and we do get on. I always thought: *I have to be there, for him and for the kids.*

If Paul did not want to speak to people, even family or guests, he would just ignore them. I would just cringe. If he was at football, playing matches or on the tours abroad, I could have people around and not feel embarrassed by that.

I did not know the full extent of what had happened to him until he spoke to the *Daily Mirror* and told in detail just how bad it had been; I had no idea it had been to that extent, though in my eyes no extent is acceptable.

It does explain how he was; Chloe and Adam suffered most because they saw verbal abuse and Chloe remembers not very nice things said about their mum. But both the girls idolise him. It was only when Paul finally went to seek help that he changed.

I went with him for that first session of counselling, to make sure that he was there, to help him. It was clearly hard for him to face up to his problems, and again, it took some courage to admit what he had become.

But then he started to mellow, and we have seen the benefit, without any doubt. Since then, we have had some of the happiest years of the marriage.

Looking back at his career, at Man City when he travelled from home to training and to and from the games, it was still early in his career and there was complete dedication. It was those years at Tottenham when he started to be a nightmare. Only now do I know that is when the drug taking really started, when I came back to Blackpool. It was hard for me in London with a young child, Adam was just starting at nursery, and Paul was out so much of the time.

Even when I came back to Blackpool, I would be worried how he would be when he came home. Eventually, long after he had stopped playing, when I had gone through so many tough times, wondering where he was, he finally owned up to it. It was around ten years ago now, when he was in his mid-40s, and he realised it was time to change. It explained many years of his behaviour, which I thought had been in drink, when he went AWOL, and we had no idea where he was.

I think he knew by then that he had to do something about it – he decided to go and get help once I had confronted him about his drugs habit, but that was the first I knew of it.

I was so naive when I look back. I had put the mood swings down to how he was – and the booze.

When he did drink in those days, he would start and not know when to stop, especially after he stopped playing. He would go away and disappear for days and I would not know where he was. He would go on lads' holidays, he did not think he had to answer to me, and if he wanted to go, he would go.

It gradually got worse after he retired from the game, there was a period when he really would just disappear.

The worst part was that I never knew where he was; I would ring around friends because I was so angry. I never got very far with that because they all stuck together, the loyalty if you like. In the worst times, Adam and I would drive around Poulton to see if we could find him, in the bars and clubs, we knew his favourite haunts.

I hated that whole thing of going out looking for him. I would never go into a pub and show myself up, or the kids. I did not want to be one of those wives who did that, I did not want to make myself look stupid.

I remember he was in a lock-in after hours once and I was very tempted to ring the police out of sheer frustration. I could not do it in the end. I imagined making the call…

"Hello, is that the police? Yes, I would like to report my husband…" It just seemed too much somehow when I said those words to myself.

•••••••

There have been so many occasions when he stormed out of the door – and ended up abroad. Missing our daughter Chloe's 16th birthday was the worst, which is 10 years ago now.

Paul came in at three or four one morning and we had a blazing row. He just said: "That's it, I'm off!" He grabbed some hand luggage and his passport, called a taxi and took an easyJet flight from Manchester to Alicante. That was the last I saw of him for days. I found out later he travelled to Denia, a small town popular with Spanish holidaymakers, where he booked himself into a nice hotel. He was on his own, although an old Blackpool colleague was living out there as well as a friend from the town, so he had some company. He would be telling them: "Bev's kicked me out again…"

He called on Chloe's birthday and when he spoke to me, he told me he was on his way to the airport to fly home. I went ballistic on the phone, telling him what I thought of him and apparently he then told the taxi driver to go around the round-about and back to the hotel, where he checked in for another five days! It's something we laugh about now, but obviously I was not happy at the time and I know Paul is not proud of what he did. We had to cancel Chloe's party. We had a big barbecue planned and it was not something I could take on alone.

I ended up buying her extra presents to compensate, getting her surprises, taking her for lunch and spending on her but really that was not what she wanted. She just wanted her party. It was so embarrassing having to cancel it, telling your own family that he was away again – and not even knowing where he had gone. You can imagine the conversation when I had to ring around all the people we had invited.

"I'm cancelling Chloe's party.

"Why?

"Paul's not here."

"Where has he gone? When will he be back?"

"I don't know, he's gone AWOL again."

AWOL became my word for his bad behaviour.

It was the fact Chloe was looking forward to it that I had found so hard. As a mother, I knew Paul's behaviour was starting to impact on the kids.

I have never smoked, never touched a drug in my life; being from a council estate, you knew people who were on it, but I am not an addictive personality and never wanted to try it.

Sometimes – and it is a funny thing to say, it is so simple – but I wondered how people knew that about other people taking drugs when they offered them out at a party or in a bar. How can you be sure when you first hand them around?

BEV'S STORY

I like a glass of wine, I might drink too much and have a hangover now and again. But taking drugs, and drinking to excess has been hard for me to understand. If I am going to see my daughter Chloe, and she wants me to help with the baby, I would not touch a drop, and not miss it.

We are one big family; we are always together with my twin sister Karen and her husband Ian, their three children Callum, Madison and Mia, and my mum Sheila. I have an older sister Melanie and brother Paul, and the impact of what I was going through was felt by us all.

My mum and Karen would tell me to leave him because they would see what I was going through with the kids. I would go to my mum and tell her about what had happened, when he went off and did not come back for days. Paul loves her, they have a great relationship and get on really well, which I know is not always what you expect with a mother-in-law.

We are incredibly close to Paul's mam and dad, they moved from Manchester to be close to us and the grandkids. Paul's mam and dad, and my mother, my sister, they would all support me in whatever choice I made, and there have been many times when I did leave him.

I would say that has happened more than a dozen times down the years. That would mean me going off to stay with my sister – and I would take the kids with me. But then, when Paul came down off the drink or drugs and everything calmed down, he would always want me to come home. I think the longest time I was away from him was about five nights. As close as I am to my twin sister, I did not feel I could stay for longer; I just had to get out of the situation.

The worst part of the drink, the drugs, when I look back

now, was the coming down. It was just horrendous for everyone around him – and usually, that meant me and the kids.

Paul would not speak and be miserable, so there was a constant atmosphere in the house. I was treading on eggshells all the time, and so were the kids.

They would come in from school, and I would usher them into the kitchen for a catch-up while he was sat on his own in the lounge. My sister knew about everything, I confided in her, we see each other every day and support each other through all our problems.

But she also saw at first hand the impact his behaviour had on me. I was a mum doing the best for the kids and not getting any support. For long periods of the marriage, my mum and Karen were very concerned about me. It was not easy, regardless of what had happened to him.

I know with my first grandchild now, if I was in that position with my kids, I would be upset and that is how mum was. They said they would look after me. And you might not expect this, but Paul's parents were always on my side too.

For all the problems down the years – which I know can be common in any marriage – I also know we are very privileged, and never forget that. We have a lovely house here, the family comes around all the time, the kids are provided for and work with Paul in his business – we have a nice lifestyle.

When I watch the TV news and hear about all the problems around the world, I think of the army wives whose husbands go away to places like Afghanistan. They don't know if they are coming back, and you have to remember and appreciate that when you look at your own problems in life, even in the worst of times.

BEV'S STORY

When Paul went to Australia to set up his business after he stopped playing, because he was so much better by then, we did miss him more, and could not wait for him to come home.

I told the kids that he had been abused when I felt they were old enough to cope because I wanted to explain his behaviour.

They just accepted that in the end.

He did not trust anybody. Now, at long last, we know why. It has meant that we understand Paul so much better, and can appreciate everything that he has been through – and all the things he has achieved.

The marriage has been a rollercoaster at times, but I always say that if we had not stuck together, I would not have had Jade and she is such a lovely, lovely girl, we are truly blessed.

I am glad we stayed strong through it because we are in such a good place now. When you are older, you look back and wonder how we got through it all. I was from a broken marriage and although we had a wonderful upbringing, I did not want our kids to face that, so I stayed and worked at it.

We spend all our time now trying to help out as much as we can; it is lovely being a grandmother. When you have been through some hard times, you appreciate the good times that much more.

Chapter/19

SURVIVORS

Even though I did eventually come to terms with my addiction to drugs through the counselling, it did not really deal with the depression.

I had a brief spell – and it was very brief – of life 'in retirement.' I soon realised that doing nothing apart from the odd game of golf, and a few hours at the gym, was not for me.

I know only too well how hard it was for Bev and the kids when I was going through the worst of it, especially in that period when football was over for me; the days locked in a room alone; ignoring visitors when they came to call and on social occasions; it is so important to seek help.

When I read about Aaron Lennon's troubles, when he was detained under the Mental Health Act in May 2017, I thought of all the times when I have had depression and how difficult it is to get out of it. Depression can hit the richest and the poorest. It has no respect for money, or status. It is a mental illness, a chemical imbalance of the brain that I suffered throughout my time at the top, at Spurs, Liverpool, Sunderland and Stoke City.

To deal with it, I opted for a range of medication – prescribed for the past 10 years – which helps me sleep. It is designed to control my mood swings. That keeps me stable 90 per cent of the time. Nevertheless I still suffer episodes, even while writing this book. Going back to the experiences of my childhood, reliving the memories of those early years, was bound to reawaken pain locked away all that time.

Roper came back in nightmares, flashbacks; those old photos of him waiting to head off to the USA with his young side, or lining up for the Nova team shots – they took me back to the trips abroad, my old mates, my brothers' feelings of guilt.

This time, I shared how I was feeling with my wife. It was only done in the form of a text, but I wrote to her: *I don't know what's up with me, feel really low, I am trying not to take it out on anyone.* It sounds an almost trivial thing – but it is important because it shows that I have learned to share the feelings when they come now. They are bleak, strange, hard to fathom. But the fact I was able to say something this time is a sign of the progress which I have made. I would hope that reading this helps anyone who does suffer; be assured that you are not alone.

When you are little and you go through something like abuse, it is so traumatic it is almost like an 'outer body' experience – you can see yourself as if you are in the corner of a room, you rely on the instinct to survive.

I am still dealing with the feelings of being in peril, I know they may be there when I wake up in the morning. It is a sense of belonging that makes you feel safe, the feeling that people are there for you. That helps you come out the other side.

•••••••••

Preston is a lovely station, a great old building, with a high glass roof over the trains and waiting passengers far below; but it was cold and drafty as I stood on the platform ready to go to London.

I was on my way to Wembley for the first time in 25 years. There were no supporters singing 'Wem-ber-ley' this time. No Spurs banners, no England flags, no huge crowds or pre-match nerves. Yet I still had the same feelings of expectation as I readied myself for a meeting with the FA.

They had asked me and a number of other former players targeted by their paedophile coaches to a meeting at the new Wembley. Strangely, as I stood on the dimly-lit platform on that freezing December morning, under that huge windowed roof, I was getting recognised like all those years before.

The last time I had been to the home of the national game, I was running out for my England debut on September 11, 1991.

It had been quite a year for me and the old stadium. There was that first ever FA Cup semi-final there against Arsenal; my goal, Gazza's injury and all the drama of the '91 final; then my dad looking proudly on as I played for my country. This time, the looks from strangers came for a very different reason. People were coming up to me on the train, congratulating me.

"Well done, keep up the good work...I'd just like to say how courageous you are...good luck, mate, you are setting a great example..."

I was 'famous' for a whole new reason, a hero in the eyes of some, but not for scoring that goal, or playing for England; for facing up to my past. People were staring because of the recent TV coverage of the soccer abuse scandal, and my story in the national press just two weeks earlier.

In those days of frenetic media interviews in November 2016, the *Mirror's* banner front page with my old Spurs team photo had beamed out on news reports on Sky, the BBC and ITV. I was on morning television as well as the six o'clock news.

The FA had invited me for talks as I was critical of them in some of that coverage, convinced they had been 'burying their heads in the sand.'

Despite those weeks in the public eye, there was no direct contact from the people at the very top of the game and I must admit that I did feel let down. The PFA had been less than impressive in their reaction all those years ago to my drug problems. I thought the FA's inaction had been even worse in a way, and it had contributed to my derogatory remarks about those at the very top.

They covered my travel to London and I requested a seat in first class, not because I thought I should travel this way. It was just that I was receiving so much attention wherever I went, I felt a bit uncomfortable about being back in the public eye.

After retiring as a player, I had returned to a more traditional life. Yes, I was recognised now and again in certain settings, on holiday, down the pub, at the occasional charity do or golf day. Rarely, if ever, had I been at the centre of this kind of attention in public. You become self-conscious about people staring, trying to place you, then remembering the reason for the media coverage.

The first class carriages were not full, but people came up to me again, as they passed, congratulating me for my bravery in speaking out. I kept my head buried in my iPad for the entire journey consciously avoiding eye contact. The journey was only two hours, 15 minutes but felt an eternity.

SURVIVORS

Once in London, I was meeting Derek Bell, an ex-Newcastle United player abused by his former coach; David White, my old mate from Manchester City, and Ian Ackley, the Crewe Alexandra man involved in the original *Dispatches* programme on soccer abuse way back in 1997.

He gave a moving, powerful account of what had happened to him from 1979 to 1983. But his story had been largely ignored. He still felt very angry about the way he had been treated.

Ian was firmly of the belief that no one had taken it seriously all those years before. Now we had spoken out, he felt that all of a sudden people were standing up and paying attention to the terrible crimes he had talked about decades earlier.

I met David at Euston, and we were then catching the underground to Wembley, seeing Derek and Ian there. It was on that long Tube journey out to Wembley that I started to think again about my footballing days, which seemed so long ago.

It was strange really, as we arrived at Wembley Tube station. Would I remember it as it was or would the new stadium have a completely different feel?

Walking up the famous Wembley Way, I could never have imagined I would return like this, my childhood secret now public knowledge. I had fully expected to keep it buried away until my dying day.

Details of the meeting had obviously got through to the media. TV cameras and reporters awaited our arrival again, as we approached the main entrance. I refused to speak prior to the meeting. It seemed to me only right that we listened to what the FA had to say before commenting. So I found myself at the entrance to the new stadium. The twin towers had long gone, but the giant arch was impressive.

The only thing that had not changed from quarter of a century before was my open collar. It may not have been a cup final suit this time; there was none of that intense noise, but, as ever, there was no tie. I smiled to myself as I was always in trouble at my former clubs for refusing to wear one. Typically, I could never give a reason why – it just never felt comfortable for me.

I wasn't nervous exactly as we stood there in the huge Wembley reception hall. But I thought: *I'm not going to have long to say my piece here. I'd better not waste a single minute.*

We had to sign in, before being directed to the fourth floor, where the FA had all their offices.

The new team line-up was a very different one from before. But you could still sense a certain tension. There were few words as we waited, surrounded by posters of the England team, promoting the kit, the latest fixtures, ticket sales. Our minds were on very different times; the teams of our youth, the buried memories which we now had to explore once again, the men who had ruined lives.

The FA boardroom was as impressive as that famous Wembley pitch. There is a sense of history still about the place, the iconic images from games past, the glory of 1966 and all the FA Cup finals.

That long, light oak table sat 12-15 of the top brass at the FA. Without thinking, I sat at the very top, with David White to my left and Ian and Derek on my right. The seat right next to me was empty; five minutes later, I found myself beside the 'Head Honcho' of the FA, the chairman Mr Greg Clarke.

It was quite a line-up of officials – it took me back in some ways to the contract negotiations I handled single-handedly throughout my career. This was a very different meeting – and there was no Derek the coach driver this time!

Clarke was joined by the director of safeguarding for the FA Sue Ravenslaw, Dr Elly Hanson, a psychologist who specialises in the field of trauma and who works for the FA on a consultancy basis, and an administration clerk who was there to take the minutes.

Sue chaired the meeting asking everyone around the table to introduce themselves. I detected a slight dig at the fact comments had been made in the national press criticising the FA, which I believe were aimed at me.

She apologised for the ordeal we had endured. She wanted to reassure us that the FA took our disclosures very seriously, and explained that they had been advised not to contact us, due to the on-going police investigations.

Greg Clarke explained that he was sorry for our experiences and said that the FA would support us, including our families, describing recent media coverage as 'overwhelming.' Only three months into his tenure, he admitted it was the most challenging time he was ever likely to endure.

Then came the time to introduce myself.

I had considered during all the introductions what I was there to say. I spoke slowly and deliberately.

"I am Paul Stewart. I am a former professional footballer. I played for Blackpool, Manchester City, Tottenham Hotspur, Liverpool, Sunderland and other clubs during my career. I was abused by my youth football coach for four years..."

After a long pause, I then explained that I was not there to criticise, but that I made no apologies for my press statement. In fact, I referred to how the statement had instigated the meeting, and that it was disappointing that such a comment was the reason I was sat there.

My only focus now was to try and help other victims.

Much had already changed since the 1970s but I told them: "I want to help you with future safeguarding, to help identify any shortfalls, to try and eradicate the possibilities of this ever happening again." Ultimately, I felt this was the chance to set a precedent, for the FA to achieve something positive from what had gone before.

I have been back to Wembley for several meetings since, looking out over the halfway line, occasionally glancing over to the spot where I scored my FA Cup final goal, allowing myself a little smile.

We are making real progress with the FA, targeting a victory in a challenge of a very different kind: making the game better for future generations.

And we are almost there.

A new safeguarding blueprint is taking shape which will be introduced within football. The ultimate aim is for it to be adapted and applied to all regulated children's activities. Unfortunately we have yet to persuade the government to endorse our project. We await that response with interest.

However, the Football Association has agreed that it will still restructure safeguarding procedures within the game, from grassroots to professional level, and that is no mean feat. We want mandatory reporting introduced in all organisations, and we believe we can make that happen.

FA chairman Mr Clarke assured us, right from that first meeting: "I won't let you down." And he has kept his word.

Our aim moving forward is to introduce a system that gives

parents or guardians the confidence to be able to leave their children with any organisation.

Parents should not have to worry about leaving their children in the hands of monsters, waiting to prey on them behind the cloak of a coach or manager role. Parents need peace of mind.

•••••••

'One Paul Gascoigne, there's only one Paul Gascoigne...'

When the legends were reunited to say farewell to White Hart Lane in May 2017, there was one man missing.

The fans didn't forget him and it was touching when they chanted Gazza's name while former players took to the pitch to wave to the fans after Tottenham's final game of the season against Manchester United.

I was honoured to be invited and it was a privilege to be there, to see some old friends and to say my goodbyes to a stadium that held so many happy memories for me. I was as close to Gazza as anyone at Spurs and it was a shame, but no surprise, that he wasn't there.

These days, Gazza still gets in touch. I can be in a meeting when I hear my phone go.

'NO CALLER ID' flashes up and I know exactly who it is and why he is calling. I know it is Gazza and he is back on the drink. If I can't take the call due to work or if I'm with someone, then I may get a text.

When he has been in rehab then it worries me. He will text me his new number, and I know there will be times when I cannot keep taking the calls because he is incomprehensible.

The calls may start with: "I love you, you are like my brother" to the other extreme, threats of violence, threats to knock me out.

I can get annoyed because when he calls he will say things like: "I am going to end my life. I am 300 miles away and you cannot do anything about it." The calls can be at three, four, five in the morning; you fear it could be bad news so you take the call and you have that desperate realisation that he has been drinking again.

I know better than anyone that you can't subject your body to that sort of abuse. It means you will pay a price.

When Paul is in drink, when he calls, I think he wants me to be a father to him. There are so many things I want to say, but under the circumstances, it is often difficult.

I want to say: "Look at me; I have managed to kick the drugs habit and don't end up feeling like I need to drink. What made you great was your ability to deal with any situation. You did it after battling with your knee injury for all that time. I cannot remember you ever letting anything beat you in your entire career – why are you letting this beat you now? If you played pool you wanted to win, if you played table tennis it was always in the belief you would not be beaten.

"I cannot believe you are giving in to this. You are a different man in drink, Paul, and when you call, you are too far gone to listen.

"I hope you listen to me now."

Chapter 20

JUSTICE

Just two weeks after my first interview and that decision to go public, there was devastating news not just for me, but for all of Frank Roper's victims. Strangely, it was harder for my family to bear than it was for me. But it was not the ending that any of us had wanted.

We learned that Frank Roper had died in St Ann's Hospice, Heald Green, Stockport, on September 13th, 2005, from prostate cancer. Roper died in a hospice near his former home, as sad and lonely a figure in his final years as he had been for his entire adult life.

He had returned to the UK from Thailand to see his own mother after she fell ill in Stockport, where Roper had worked – and abused kids – for so many years. Roper was then diagnosed with cancer, and presumably elected to remain in the UK for NHS treatment, then palliative care.

He ended his days in St Ann's, part of the largest hospice group in Manchester, set in leafy grounds not far from his old home.

The records state that he was aged 69. It was his brother who offically notified the authorities. We approached that brother for his thoughts while researching this book.

I had mixed feelings about going to see him.

As I sat outside his house, an imposing property in an affluent suburb, I wondered: *What would I say to the family of the man who abused me every day for for four years? What words could I find to express my feelings about the serial paedophile who escaped justice? How would they feel about the most disturbing revelation imaginable about a close family member, more than a decade after his death?*

In the end, they did not want to see me. Roper had kept his activities hidden from everyone, including his nearest relatives. But we learned some more details of Roper's secret life, his death, his final years.

Roper's family had lost touch after his departure for Thailand, which is believed to have been in the early '90s. We visited the house which Roper used to share with his mother – again in Stockport – when I first met him.

I remembered all those visits there, locked away deep in my psyche, when Roper had kept me waiting in the passenger seat of his red Fiat as he went inside.

The dutiful son looking after his elderly mother. Making sure she had all she needed – shopping, money, her bills paid and sorted. All with his latest victim sitting outside, a little lad in his footy kid, his feet swinging, not touching the ground of the footwell in his car.

Here was yet another side to the monster which I had not properly considered before. He was somebody's loving son, somebody's footy-mad brother, somebody's mysterious uncle living thousands of miles away in the Far East. He was all these things to all the different people in his life.

Now, to his grown-up victims, he was the dark shadow in the corner of their minds: waiting to strike again when they least expected it – in flashbacks and nightmares, or on some old TV footage showing the days of their childhood, the glimpse of an old-fashioned tracksuit in the corner of a screen. Devastating lives for years to come, long after he had been seen in person for the last time. Long after his death.

I was never allowed in to see his mother and you can understand why; it may have led to awkward questions about what I was doing with him, a kid of 11 in his football kit.

The death of Roper was harder for my family to bear than it was for me.

It sounds strange to say it now, but after the initial searches proved fruitless, even when the police got involved, I had guessed he would be dead, not so much a fear as intuition. There had been a faint hope that he might still be alive to face justice. But it was just too late. It meant the serial abuser of young children would never face a court of law.

Speaking about him now, even going back over the graphic details of the abuse, has not hit me emotionally as you might expect. I can never take away the damage he did not just to me but countless other victims over decades. Those are the long term effects of abuse.

I had to deal with it growing up, and its impact remained long after it had stopped. But his death did not really change anything for me. It was never about revenge or justice. It would not have changed what he did to me even if he did end up behind bars.

If you look at the cases of other notorious paedophiles, so many of their victims are amazed when they deny their heinous crimes. Sometimes they face court many years, even decades after the offences were committed.

But what makes anyone think a child sex offender is going to act honourably once they have been caught?

There are so many victims who may find it difficult to help others because they are still so angry themselves. If you still have those emotions, that fury, it can take over your life.

I had to deal with those feelings throughout my playing career, and still play at the top level. Crossing the white line on a Saturday was the ultimate escape.

The decision to go public was about supporting others, backing those who had waived their anonymity – and helping anyone who had been through what we had suffered. I wanted to forget Roper.

My wife Bev was concerned that digging up the past might be too much, re-living that pain all over again. I tried to reassure my family: *It doesn't matter that he's dead…I buried him a long time ago.*

I knew there were other people out there who were abused by him. I had met them, spoken with them, some lived close to my own home.

Another grim reality to ponder: I knew there were parents who were aware that he had abused their children. But I had spoken with the game's governing bodies, the FA, PFA, and gave a detailed account to the police.

As with all the other victims who waived their right to anonymity, going public was the only way I could bring some justice to bear.

JUSTICE

It helped the victims who found the strength to come forward for the first time, and to tell their loved ones.

And it meant everyone knew Roper for what he really was. Not the benevolent coach taking kids on tournaments around the world, guiding them to professional careers.

But a serial abuser of children.

••••••••

I still find it hard to comprehend, all these years later, how Roper evaded justice over decades, how he got away with it for so long.

We now know that Lancashire Police had a chance to bring him before the courts in April 2003 – more than two years before he died.

One of the victims who contacted me after I went public in 2016 was from my own town of Blackpool. He came forward to the authorities to say he had been attacked twice in the 1980s, around four years after I got out of Roper's car and escaped his clutches for the last time. The reasons for not pursuing a prosecution were 'under review' in 2017. They will be of great interest to Roper's countless victims.

Roper had travelled and worked in Bangkok for more than a quarter of a century, targeting children there while on tour with the Nova youth team, en route to tournaments in New Zealand, throughout the '70s and '80s.

By the time of his death, he had abused children over at least 20 years in England; on tours to America, Ireland, and New Zealand, and then, in the final years of his life – well into his 60s – around the seedy bars and clubs of Bangkok.

DAMAGED/20

Former Leeds United and Hull City player Jamie Forrester is another player who has bravely come forward. He watched in horror as Roper abused a Thai boy on one tour there.

On New Year's Eve, 2016, Forrester, now 42, told the *Sunday People* how Roper took him and other boys on an all-expenses paid, five-day football tour of Thailand in the mid-'80s.

"One night during the trip we went out to watch Thai boxing, Forrester said. "Roper had a young Thai boy, about 11 or 12, the same age as us, sitting on his knee.

"I can remember thinking at the time: *What's going on?* but I was only 11, I didn't feel like I could say anything. The Thai boy came back with us to our hotel and because we were all staying in the same room he came in to the room and we all got into bed. The lights went out and the next thing Roper started molesting the Thai boy and then began having sex with him in the bed next to us.

"I was in the bed next to him and it was happening two yards away. It was terrifying and I felt like it was all completely out of my control. I was very scared.

"Me and the other boys all lay in absolute silence. There was no way any of us could have done or said anything. I felt like I had to pretend I wasn't there and it was like we were frozen statues.

"In the morning he was still laid there in bed with Roper."

Forrester claims that Roper was at the centre of a paedophile ring that preyed on young footballers. "Roper used to talk very often about another man and his junior team. He would say things like, 'You think you're good? They're better than you, they'll kick your arse.' He was always talking about this guy, who I know now was a notorious paedophile.

"A match was arranged between the two teams. I played in the match with others who went on to be professional. Shortly afterwards the other man made contact with my parents to invite me to his house for the weekend. Thankfully my parents declined because of rumours about him."

If you look at the police statistics for the region and tally them with the period Roper was active as a paedophile – from the early '70s, to his time in Thailand which came to an end around 40 years later – there must be hundreds of victims. Not all will have found the courage to come forward.

Someone who did, Scott Ramsbottom, 44, was the man who went to police in Blackpool in 2003, when Roper was still alive. Scott, a dad of one, felt 'vindicated' when he read my story. It showed that he had been telling the truth.

He told the *Sunday Mirror:* "I am angry that the police did nothing. He should have spent the last years of his life in prison." Scott was spotted by Roper as he prowled the seafront in Blackpool in the mid-'80s.

He recalled: "He would give kids money to play the fruit machines. After a while, he offered to take me to Blackpool games. He said he'd get me in for free in the directors' box. Afterwards he'd take a group of us to the arcades or a restaurant in town."

His account followed a sickeningly familiar pattern. "He'd give us all lifts home in his van and would be touching up whoever was in the front seat next to him," recalled Scott.

"He offered me a job in his shop. He said he'd take me to see it but it would be a sleepover. I had to ask my mum for permission. Frank drove a van that was always full of sports gear and he'd give me some."

Scott says they stayed in a house near Manchester airport – probably the same house I visited in Stockport – and he woke during the night to find Roper in his bed abusing him.

"I was scared. I knew what he was doing was wrong and I felt disgusted," he said. He told Roper to stop and pushed his hand away.

"I was too frightened to say anything to anyone," he says. "I guess I just tried to forget about it. Frank never spoke about it. I went to his shop the next day and he carried on treating me to presents and money."

A few months later Scott was invited to Manchester again and reluctantly accepted. "This time we stayed in a hotel. I was worried. The same thing happened. When I went to bed he got in beside me and started touching me again. I tried to push him off but he just carried on. I was frightened. I couldn't do anything."

In April 2003, at 31 years of age, he eventually found the strength to go to the police. He said: "I guess they didn't believe me. And they didn't want to open that can of worms."

Scott was back in touch with officers after my interview.

Lancashire Police confirmed they were aware of a historic complaint and were reviewing it 'to see if anything further can be done.'

For all his victims, there are questions on how he got away with it for so long. The answers are important not just for us but for future generations of young children who will play the game we all love.

Chapter 21

A NEW LIFE

Wednesday, March 1, 2017

I feel like an expectant father again as I make the short drive from home to Blackpool Victoria Hospital. Jade, my youngest daughter, is with me. Chloe, my other daughter, is expecting her first child – and my first grandchild.

I feel the same tension and anxiety as I did at my son Adam's birth.

We had agreed not to go to the hospital all together as we felt it would have been too much for Chloe. So Bev stayed and was giving me updates on the phone at home.

I was walking back and forth puffing on an e-cigarette and talking to Jade about what might happen, going through all the different possibilities in my mind.

When I heard that there were complications and a 'crash team' had gone into the delivery suite, I could wait no more and I made my way down to the hospital.

It was one of the longest journeys of my life.

I have never felt such tension, such raw nerves, as we park up by the clock tower and race into the modern new building. I am so worried about Chloe, my mind is racing about what might go wrong; it is irrational but I cannot help it – I am desperate to get inside.

As I arrive, there are about 15 nurses and doctors in the room; a team for the baby and another for Chloe.

Even when I get there, Bev can only give a brief update before she goes back through the doors to the delivery suite.

She tells me that Chloe may need a blood transfusion and I am panicking again as I walk up and down, in the bright, white light of the hospital corridor. It is impossible to describe the feelings of concern, inexplicable really; I could not settle until I knew she was through it.

All that anxiety disappears as I see Bev.

"Congratulations Granddad!" she says. She breaks the happy news that little Sienna has entered the world and Chloe is fine, albeit after a forceps delivery. The baby is so cute and we all feel so relieved. It is a feeling of sheer elation.

I never saw myself running around *Boots* buying baby milk and nappies again.

But here I am – and never happier. People ask me how I am doing; an old school friend in Poulton market, around Blackpool, at work, and I cannot wait to tell them the news.

Since the birth, Chloe has had the sort of issues so often seen with a first baby. She was not sleeping well, Sienna was always hungry, and of course there came a time when her partner was going back to work.

So she came to stay with us, to get some rest, and I would often find myself with Sienna in my arms at first light; Bev staying up all night to help with the feeds while Chloe built up her strength.

It is a new life for both of us – Bev is even more excited than me about the new arrival, if that's possible – and we are both keen to help as much as we can.

It means running around *Tesco* for emergency supplies every now and again. Nipping to the chemists if there is something specific the baby needs. Just being around to give an extra pair of hands now and again. Chloe has been grateful, and we have all loved having her around.

Her partner is Matt Walwyn, the son of York City's late, great striker Keith. He was one of their all-time record goalscorers and by a strange quirk of fate, replaced me at Blackpool when I left for Manchester City.

Matt is a useful player too – he scored twice in the 2008 FA Vase final at Wembley, when he was still a 17-year-old A-Level student. He came on to score in the 84th minute, and again in injury time, turning a 1-0 deficit against Lowestoft into a 2-1 victory for Kirkham & Wesham. Another time, he scored two late goals in AFC Fylde's 2-2 draw at Clitheroe that won a pools punter more than £3 million! His dad Keith died at just 47 years of age in 2003 while undergoing a heart operation. We have done our best to be there for Matt and Chloe.

In recent months, Chloe has opened up to me about her experiences growing up.

During her teenage years I was going through some of the worst phases of the addiction to cocaine. There were the lost days recovering in the lounge at home, the door shut, in a world of my own; the stick she got at school over her dad being a 'coke head.' She remembers me 'going off the rails completely' when she was around 13 and Bev driving around the pubs in Poulton to try and get me home. Jade, still young by the time that I got off the drugs, was sheltered from the worst of it, but Chloe and Adam would get in the car with their mother to come and look for me.

Chloe told me her friends would ask what was going on at home. Her best friend Lucy would say: "What's the matter?" trying to be kind, to help. But she could not tell her about the constant battles caused by my 'lost days' through the drink and drugs. When I disappeared abroad and missed her 16th birthday, she remembered it well:

> You called me from Spain and said: 'Chloe, it's your dad.' I did not even know where you were, your voice was all hoarse. As soon as you rang me and I heard you speaking, I started crying. But I was never angry, it was just more upsetting than anything. You were not around for my birthday so just hearing your voice was enough to set me off. We did not know where you were until you called.

Despite it all, Chloe would defend me to the last, and told her friends: "He has been a good dad, I would never change him. I never saw any of your dads and thought I want one like them, it has always been the case."

After that first *Mirror* interview, Chloe found a quote. 'People don't believe in heroes, but they have not met my dad.' It was shared by Chloe and Jade with all their friends on social media, on Facebook, the way kids communicate these days. It was very poignant for me.

Jade also told me I did not realise that I still 'hold the family together', despite all my problems and that I had been there not just for Bev and the kids, but my brothers, my mum and dad. It was Bev who took me to that first crucial counselling session; after that, I could call someone when I felt the need, and go down to seek help. The shame of what was happening to the kids was another big, big reason to change.

I was mortified when Adam found a coke sachet in my jacket. He took it to Bev to ask about it, but he was old enough then to know what it was. I felt nothing but utter shame, my son finding that in his father's coat.

On top of all this was the fact that I couldn't show any love or emotion to my own children. Chloe told me she never felt able to come to me for a hug when she was growing up.

It is a cycle I am determined to break with her little girl Sienna. The arrival of my granddaughter marks a fresh chance for a life free of the problems which have so affected mine. Sienna coming along feels like a new chapter in my life, a turning point, a ray of hope and happiness.

Typically, like the rest of my life, there was nothing straight-forward, there was drama even in the delivery suite. But it all came right in the end.

••••••••

My life now has seen so many changes.

There has been such a transformation in life outside of work, a public role if you like, as a result of coming forward.

It is one which I could never have foreseen back in 2016, when I made the decision to go public.

You learn so much when going through an experience like this – including plenty about yourself.

My parents told of my 'year of silence' as I dealt with Roper's daily abuse; I now realise I had to completely disassociate to get through it, to switch off from the trauma of what I was going through, an almost primeval instinct to survive.

Roper's threats to kill my family members were all too real for a kid at 11 years old.

In response, I completely shut down emotionally.

While I still saw friends at football, and still went to school, it became easier to say nothing, knowing it would be my parents' worst nightmare if they were to find out. As a victim, the abuse was placed in a separate part of my mind. I had to deal with the feeling that I was going to die; at that age, the feelings and fears must have been so overwhelming.

Football was my salvation in so many ways. Though I was only targeted by Roper as a result of my love of the game, just getting out and playing saved my life. It enabled me to live without constantly looking over my shoulder at the past.

At the same time, as I made it in the game, the non-stop life-style of the professional footballer meant it became an escape; that I did not face up to the issues in my life, the legacy of the abuse, emotionally and psychologically; football was my way of avoiding that. It was a vicious circle.

My football family also shielded me from the realities of my life as an abuse victim. You spend so much time with your team-mates. During the season you can be together, travelling around to matches – especially abroad – virtually 24/7.

I tried to 'manage' those two sides of my life as best as I could during my playing days. I knew no other way than silence and strength, but keeping everything inside would only make matters worse.

The adrenalin rush of happiness at the first hit of coke meant I could forget what had happened in a way I had never been able to before. Looking back, I wonder if there was also an element of self-destruct.

Now I ask myself if I felt the guilt shared by so many victims; the endless questioning of 'why did it happen to me?' and the self-blame. There is an inexplicable 'guilt' at doing nothing in that situation, even when you are trapped by your abuser, a man mercilessly exploiting a boy of 11.

Those feelings of shame and guilt were what I had intended to keep locked away forever. You cannot see them on the outside. People do not know they are there.

They came out through the anger which was seen right through my early football career. At Blackpool, I was banned for matches, sent off, constantly in trouble with the authorities; it was a pattern repeated at other clubs. That anger would not subside really until I reached my 40s, when the therapy and counselling helped me to understand my feelings.

When I finished playing, my depression came to the surface again. There was a huge void in my life. The comfort and camaraderie of the dressing room was taken away from me. It's not something that you can adapt to straight away. There is no one there; no manager, no backroom staff, no experts to advise you on what to do. It is over, and you have to find your own way, which is not that easy.

Professional footballers get far more advice these days, and so they should. I know some players say we are treated like a piece of meat at times and that is especially true come the end of your career – when you reach your sell-by date. When I finished, there were still so many unresolved issues in my life. But I had still not reached the stage where I was ready to do anything about them. I suppose I was still emotionally immature.

The easiest choice is always not to confront your situation. Football couldn't help me do that anymore, but drugs could. When I eventually started my business, that, too, became a focus, a way of avoiding key issues.

So, even in my retirement from football, after almost 20 years together, and three wonderful children, I was not at the stage where I could tell my wife that I loved her. I found it hard to put my arms around the kids and express how I felt.

In many ways, the interview with the *Mirror* was a turning point in my life; but I should have spoken out so much earlier, a long, long time ago.

I think speaking out, telling the world, has helped in some way. That is what people around me say; it is almost as if a weight has been lifted. It's as if there was a heaviness, a burden deep in my soul. Other victims will know immediately what I mean; you carry it, hidden away. At least that secrecy is gone now.

Has it helped to alleviate the shame? I don't know.

Once you find the courage to talk about it, there is a release. I think you do feel different somehow. Not only can you talk about it for the first time, but people can speak to you, advise you, try and help you. I am not saying that it is for everyone. But it must be worth considering if you are carrying a secret, as I did for all those years.

Going public hasn't cured everything, far from it. At least people now recognise what I have been through. I hope, above all, that it helps them to understand me; and to understand my behaviour in the past.

It is your own character, your self-worth, that is at the heart of the legacy of abuse.

If you go through a traumatic experience – and it does not matter how old you are – you re-live it later in life, again and again. You are still dealing with it as an adult; it goes around and around in your head, it does not magically go away. Like a soldier returning from war, you can be traumatised for a lifetime; in your dreams, the flashbacks which may come back years later, you are back in that situation of danger, and it is as real as it was before.

The solid bedrock of my family, my loved ones, the people who care for me, got me through.

In football, in the dressing room, I know that I had found a place where I belonged. I have found that again, right where it always was; at home, now with the little granddaughter who is lighting up all our lives.

•••••••

Physically, after the heart operation in February 2017, I feel much better, and mentally too.

My business has been a success, which makes me proud. When I started out, it was with the purchase of a £20,000 firm selling advertising space in doctors' surgeries.

It now has a £5m turnover but we are looking to double that and take on more staff, create more jobs, and expand here and abroad. We have around 1500-2000 clients worldwide, but that grows every week; there have been some ups and down in the past, but we have just done our biggest installations ever in this country, so you have to keep on looking forward.

My football career seems like another world to me now. As you've read, it wasn't all sweetness and light. In fact, with the odd, very rare exception, most players will have as many lows as highs in the game. When I finished football, it was a sense of relief more than anything. I realised my time had passed.

People say that being a footballer is the best job in the world, like being a film star. Of course, not everyone knows the reality and what you have been through to make it. The abuse I suffered happened by chance, through no fault of my own. I didn't let it beat me. Nothing deterred me in the pursuit of my dream to be a professional footballer.

I was rewarded with some brilliant memories. I know that my family are proud of what I achieved in the game. I played with and against some brilliant players; worked under some great man managers (Sam Ellis, Terry Venables and Peter Reid among them) and experienced moments of sheer joy like winning the FA Cup and playing for England.

Above all else, I look back and remember the 'five to three buzz.' Standing in the tunnel on a matchday, the flutter of nerves in the pit of my stomach; the shaft of bright light in the distance leading to a packed stadium and lush, green turf; a sea of colour and swirling noise. The chance to be a hero, to mean something to someone, if only for 90 minutes.

No one can take those memories away. They are mine. They remain as clear in my mind as if they were yesterday, and they will stay with me forever.

Through it all, my amazing wife Bev, my children, my parents, brothers, friends and family have got me through; I really would not be alive to tell the tale without them, and to them I will be forever grateful.

Despite everything, I don't want people to think I am the saddest man; the darkness is not there 24/7. Only now have I come to think that the abuse happened to me because I am strong enough to deal with it. These days, I feel like I have been given another chance. I must make the most of the different life that lies in front of me.

Do I have any regrets from first kicking a ball as a starry-eyed young lad on a patch of grass outside a house in Wythenshawe? Do I wish I had never known what football was? That I had answered a different calling in life?

Well, sometimes, we have no choice. We follow our hearts. The greatest evil can lie hidden, waiting to ambush us as we take the first steps on our chosen path.

It may have taken 52 years for me to find a reason to tell it but I know that this story will help others. I hope anyone struggling with the ordeal of abuse and its aftermath can realise that you can come out the other side.

You may be damaged, but you can find a better life.

MY LETTER TO YOU

Dear X,

I am writing to you as a fellow victim of abuse, someone who has experienced what I have.

I don't want you to see this book as the end; more a beginning.

I hope that telling my story has inspired you.

I suffered in silence for 41 years, and unfortunately the impact of the abuse manifested itself in many forms, most of which I have depicted throughout my life story.

I was left void of emotion, and unable to show any kind of love to those closest to me. At times I showed the opposite emotion to the one I intended to express. I made my family suffer in the way I behaved because I simply could not communicate in a normal way. The pain and suffering I caused for my family is something I will regret for the rest of my life, but at least I have a chance to revisit that now and to try and make some amends.

DAMAGED/A MESSAGE

The journey I have been on since I came forward to tell my story has made me realise that you can move on and survive. It is possible. No matter how dark the tunnel, there is a way through to the other side. I am proof of that. I am here, I feel strong and yes, I enjoy life, even if those moments of happiness do not always last.

I still suffer from those awful events from my childhood, but I have learned to cope, to manage. Growing old brings many things – not all good! – but one thing it brings is perspective; the ability to stand back, take time and choose the way you react to situations and moods. I am 52 and I have that perspective now but whatever your age, you can learn to control the emotions that are threatening to destroy you.

The pain never goes away but if you let it, it can consume your everyday life. I know that there are many who have suffered in that way.

My message to you is simple: You can change, you can control your life. Do not let yourself become a hostage to darkness. Easier said than done, I know, but it is possible. Although I did not realise it at the time, I allowed what happened to me to change my character, and not for the better.

You are different. You can change.

I hope that you can find a way to move on from the pain and suffering.

My thoughts are with you, so please don't suffer in silence as I did, seek whatever help you my need, even if that is just talking to someone you love.

A few words can change a life. They did for me.

Paul

Testimonies

WHAT THEY SAY

I can walk out there with my head held high because he is so very brave. We have our two young girls and my son, and all the members of my family feel very proud of him.

Bev Stewart, full-time mum,
Paul's wife of 29 years

Looking back, I did some amazing things with Dad which I just did not really think about when I was growing up.

My first love was music and I got a little guitar when I was two or three and I used to play it for the Tottenham lads. I was never very shy and Dad used to get them all around and I would play guitar and sing for them.

It would be fair to say that my taste in music has changed a fair bit since then because it was all '90s pop songs and I used to get up and sing Jason Donovan numbers, which is what you want to do at three years old. I like to think I had half an eye on Kylie Minogue! It must be something about Australia – my dad loves a bit of karaoke as well. When he went to work there for a few months after he had finished playing, there was a bar on the Southbank in Sydney and he sang the Elvis song American Trilogy. I got up and sang with him, then sat straight back down again!

We were up there on the stage in the pub, it went down really well. We got such a good reception that Dad went around shaking people's hands which was very funny. He has a thing about Elvis, he still gets up and does a turn now and again.

I am a big Liverpool fan. I was only little when he signed for them – I was about five years old – but I remember going in and just kicking the ball around with Robbie Fowler, David James, Razor Ruddock. They were all great at making me feel welcome and they always had a lot of time for me.

When you think of who they were and how important training was at that level it was very good of them to do that, but for me it was like a kick about with my mates. I did not really recognise the magnitude of that as a child – it would be like having a kick about with Daniel Sturridge and the big stars now. It was crazy – just like playing with your mates, except for me, it was the Liverpool first team.

I also met Kenny Dalglish when Dad was playing for Sunderland. We saw him in a hotel in Durham and he got me a signed ball, he was manager at Newcastle United so it had all their players' autographs on there, and I met John Barnes around that time, two Liverpool FC all-time greats. Kenny was really friendly. I remember fans later telling me about him going to all the funerals of the Hillsborough victims and just thinking that was a mark of the man, paying his respects with all the families like that. He was brilliant with me and it is another great memory of growing up. It's funny but I don't even think I told my mates about that, it was just a part of my life. I did not see it as anything special or different.

There are a lot of negative comments at school when you are the son of a famous footballer. I had the odd scuffle as a result but it subsided when I started hitting people. If they had a go, I had to look after myself. I remember talking to Dad about it and he just said: "If it gets too bad son, hit them," which I think was fair enough back then. He is a chip off the old block if you look at his dad Bert, my granddad, and that is the way I went after that.

I have noticed a real change in Dad since he spoke about what happened to him in childhood. He is not drinking as much. He is not as quiet as he once was. There is a difference there definitely, and I do think about it when I am going through any tough times in my own life.

With my niece Sienna, you can see that he is really enjoying being a granddad; he is doing a lot more about the house, which I have noticed because I am back there at the moment. He is babysitting on Saturday nights and he is really enjoying that. He is making sacrifices and that has just happened in a way because he was always so busy with football when we were little, but you can see this new life is really important to him.

I am very proud of how he had handled going public about the abuse, athough it was very difficult, there were a lot of memories for me to process at the time, and it was hard to take all that in. I had not known the detail of what happened to him, but I feel like I understand him much better now.

DAMAGED

There is a connection where we can talk about things and help each other, that is my experience of it. Now we all know what he really went through, all those years ago and in his life since then, it means we can understand him so much more.

Adam Stewart, Paul's son

Paul told me about what had happened to him before he went public. I found it so hard to come to terms with.

I never suspected Frank Roper. He took us both on a trip to Ireland when I was around 15 years old. I made so many good friends, I went to Ireland to see them on my own afterwards and Roper used to drop me off at the airport. He made a sarcastic remark about me having a bomb on me at the height of the Troubles with the IRA, and I always remember a security guard gave me such a dirty look. He would try to be funny, but there was nothing beyond that. When they went training, I thought it was with the team, not Roper with Paul on his own.

That is what was so hard about finding out about the abuse all those years later. I had nightmares. It really hit me hard. I blamed myself for not noticing – I don't blame him one bit, nor my parents. I wish I had been there for him.

We would see Roper in the Tangerine Club at Blackpool, and he would buy us all drinks. It made my day when Paul signed for Man City. I am a big City fan. We followed him at Spurs, Liverpool, Blackpool; I went to Wembley with my dad to see him play. We are all very proud of him, even more so now we know what he went through to make it.

Anthony Stewart, Paul's eldest brother

WHAT THEY SAY

We shared a bedroom and sometimes Paul would say 'can I get in bed with you Gary?' He was scared of Frank Roper, but I had no idea back then.

I was about 14 so I had to say to Paul 'no you are too old for that now' when he asked to jump in with me. If Frank did stay, we would share the bed, but it happened after that. I was so young, I did not understand. We never suspected Roper, it was the same for all the family. He brought gifts all the time, mainly sports gear. We were helping him to sell it, to fund the Nova tours to America. I was so excited about that, to go to the US.

Paul said something about abuse when he was at Spurs and we were out drinking. We both got upset. It was a real shock, very difficult to take in. If I had known about Paul's problems with drugs, I would have helped him. Roper was a monster; we welcomed him into our home, he would buy us takeaways and have tea with us, to think of that now makes my skin crawl.

Paul carried the burden too long and in hindsight, I wonder if I should have said something all those years ago, when Roper was still alive, after Paul touched on the subject. But he asked me to keep it secret.

I am so proud of him, to play at Wembley, to play for England, is absolutely amazing. We were close growing up, like two peas in a pod. Roper should have stood up before a court to admit what he had done, not just to Paul but to all the others. I am glad he is dead because he cannot harm anyone else.

How he got to coach young kids I'll never know. Did he have any coaching badges? In those days nobody checked. Everyone was just grateful there was someone to run a team.

Gary Stewart, Paul's elder brother

I tried to sign Paul and John Barnes when they were both at Liverpool and I was manager at Man City. I just liked the way Paul got everything out of his ability, and his work ethic. That combined with his skill in midfield and up front.

When I got the job at Sunderland, and he became available, I thought that he would be ideal for me, and he was terrific. He got himself fit and he was superb around the football club. He is a real diamond, a great influence in any dressing room. We had a day out on holiday recently, he has become a good friend. He is a really good lad, and it is nice to reminisce about the old days.

When you look at what he went through, you realise what a strong character he is. In that first season at Sunderland, he was a great asset, he did a fantastic job for me. As a manager, he did everything

I asked and in football terms, he could not have given any more. I did go and meet him in Lytham and he opened up about his drugs problems and said: "I'm sorry if I have let you down."

I said: "Look Paul, you have never let me down, you have been absolutely outstanding." It was difficult for him to confide but he wanted to get it off his chest and I told him he did a great job, because that really was the case.

When you have got a big squad of players, you need to look after them differently, as a manager you have to get the best out of them. There are different ways of doing that and I will have fall outs with players but you move on. Nowadays that is more difficult, but no matter what the era, football needs to be fun and your players have to be enjoying the game.

Paul always brought that sense of enjoyment. Show me a

happy dressing room, and I will show you a team with a chance of winning things. The fans in the North East were brilliant with me and I have some great memories of nights out there – in Newcastle, even though they would call me 'monkey's heed' – in Sunderland, and in Yarm where I lived. It is a fantastic part of the world, and we had some great times together there.

Peter Reid, former Sunderland manager

I always got on really well with Stewie. He was in the team when I made my Liverpool debut and I was in the team when he played his last game for Liverpool. I was a bit in awe of him when I was a kid because he was the life and soul of the squad. I did not know how much he was suffering and I feel bad he had to carry that alone.

I honestly believe he has an awful lot of football people behind him and unequivocal support in trying to create lasting change. Most of all, I hope he realises just how much his courage can help so many other people. He was always a warrior on the pitch, brave and strong – and now he is showing the same qualities in a much more important fight.

Robbie Fowler, former Liverpool team-mate

I salute Paul Stewart for so bravely revealing his personal tragedy. The physical abuse he and others suffered was certainly more extreme and prolonged than my ordeal. I cannot be sure that I would have his courage.

David White, former Manchester City team-mate

The lad came through despite everything he went through. The fact Paul went on to achieve all that he achieved in the game says all you need to know about him. I always thought midfield for England was the easy way out – he could have been an international goal scorer up front. I am not sure how many people came forward after Paul's interview, but I know there was a lot who did. That shows what Roper got away with. Paul has made sure that everyone knows what he was, and has helped those who had not come forward before. Without him, they may not have had the strength to do it.

Sam Ellis, former Blackpool manager

There were tears when I read Paul's story, I was really moved by his account and I have only got heartfelt praise in the way that he is trying to help others. This has caused so much destruction and upset in the personal lives of the victims. When Paul spoke about his suicidal thoughts, it made me think of the many young players who never made it as professionals and are no longer with us. One victim took his life at 30. There will be so many others.

Ex-Sheffield Utd player Andy Woodward

I was totally shocked when Paul went public about the abuse which he had suffered in childhood. I had no inclination that had happened to him, he had never mentioned it to anyone.

There is no doubt his story was instrumental in so many others coming forward and starting off the whole process of the police investigation. He was always a strong voice in the dressing room, someone who was respected and admired. By the time we played together at Sunderland, he had been to big clubs like Spurs, and Liverpool, he had played for England, scored in an FA Cup final and achieved so much in the game. He arrived at Sunderland around the same time as me and Niall Quinn and while he did not volunteer advice all the time, he would speak his mind and say what he thought was not working, and when it needed to be said.

Out of all my ex-team-mates, Stewy is one of the funniest people you could ever wish to meet off the pitch and that is why we have spent so much time together socially, and kept in touch. He really has to be admired for what he has done. It takes a great deal of courage, but because of him, so many other victims were inspired to reveal what happened to them for the first time, and so many abusers will be brought to book. He may be respected as a footballer first and foremost but he has gone to achieve so much outside of the game.

Tony Coton, former Sunderland team-mate

I have buried those memories for so many years, but they would still come to the surface. Every time I saw abuse on TV, on the news, or an item about the Savile inquiry, it came into my mind again and would stay there for days. It affected me way back then because I could not hug my mum, I became very cold and my parents noticed. I have never told them, right to this day. That is the message. You have to talk about it, and I greatly admire Paul for telling his story.

Ex-professional footballer, a victim of Frank Roper

I knew Frank Roper when I was a player at Blackpool. He was the official photographer when we went to tournaments with the youth team. I was only 16 or 17 at the time, so you would be talking about the 1969/70 season. That was 15 years before Paul played for the club, and six or seven years before he met him for the first time, it is frightening when you think about it.

Then he worked his way in at Blackpool, he got his feet right under the table and was coaching youth team players and became a scout for them, he would be driving the kids around, and taking them to his home. He manufactured those ways of getting into a position of trust.

I think Paul coming forward to talk about him was a tremendously courageous thing to do. I called him the day after the *Mirror* published his story; I know that I was one of many, but I could tell that he really appreciated that. I told him 'I love you to bits and you were incredibly brave to do what you did. Anything I can do to help I will do it.' He had that bottled up all those years, which made it even harder for him to speak out.

He was a man's man when he was a player. I first met him at Crystal Palace when we had a young forward called Chris Armstrong who was scoring a lot of goals. We needed an old fashioned target man and Paul came in and got us promoted. He was a great influence on the younger players, a good craic, they loved him. Chris would take a lot of stick from defenders but Paul would say to him 'don't worry, I will sort him out' and the next thing you knew he was down with claret all over his face; he did it on the quiet, no one saw him.

Paul had instant respect from the team because of where he had played and what he had done in his career. We had a good team, but he was a really good pro. He would make sure the younger lads were doing the right things and would give people a shout if we needed to do something tactically during the games. He did knit the team together. We had promotion sewn up by Easter in 1993/94, and went into the Premier League. He loved the matches, but he liked a night out afterwards as well; he came with a big reputation but he also brought real character and a great sense of humour. I really enjoyed working with him, he was good fun, and above all a brilliant pro.

Steve Harrison, ex-Crystal Palace and Wolves coach

I wanted Paul to know his story had given me the courage to tell my own family for the first time, and to thank him. I wanted to come forward because of Paul. I have had problems with drink and drugs myself and struggled to express emotion and love, even with my own children. I've told my mum who is elderly now, Paul has given me the courage to do that. Even now I think *why didn't I stop him?* but it's hard when you are so young and I was away from home at the time at a tournament. I was only 13 at the time, I was so vulnerable.

A dad-of-three, 47, also abused by Roper

So many victims have come forward after Paul spoke out.

Friend and former Spurs forward Paul Walsh

I have huge admiration for Paul. Keep fighting the cause.

Gary Stevens, ex Spurs and England star

DAMAGED

It is so sad, so courageous of all the victims who have come out to tell their stories.

Robbie Savage, ex-Wales midfielder

We reported an increase in the number of calls for help after Paul came forward, and after his appearance on Crimewatch.

The National Association for People Abused in Childhood

Morally, I find it repugnant if people suppressed crimes against children to protect their reputation.

FA chairman Greg Clarke

The players that have broken their silence to speak out about the abuse they suffered have shown immense courage. No one must ever feel they cannot or should not be able to do the same.

Crewe and Nantwich MP Edward Timpson

It's awful that some of my colleagues have suffered whilst playing the sport that I and they love. I would encourage anyone who has or is suffering from abuse to call the NSPCC help line. It's important people know there is help available and that they don't need to suffer in silence.

Wayne Rooney

STATISTICS

Paul Andrew Stewart

Born October 7, 1964.
Place of birth: Manchester.
Height: 5ft 10in (1.78m)
Position: Striker/Midfielder

Senior Career (appearances/goals):
1981–1987: Blackpool 201(56)
1987–1988: £200,000 to Manchester City 51(26)
1988–1992: £1.7m to Tottenham Hotspur 131 (28)
1992–1996: £2.5m to Liverpool 32 (1)
1994: Crystal Palace (loan)18(3)
Wolverhampton Wanderers (loan)8(2)
1995: Burnley (loan)8 (0); Sunderland (loan)2 (0)
1996–1997: Sunderland 34 (5)
1997–1998: Stoke City 21 (3)
1998–2000: Workington 55 (15)

Total 559 (139)

International honours:
1988 England U211(1)
1989–1992 England B5(1)
1991–1992 England 3(0)

FA Cup Winner and Man of the Match:
Spurs v Nottingham Forest, 91. One of very few players to have the
distinction of appearing in a north London derby, a Manchester derby, a
Merseyside derby and a North East derby.

Hall of Fame:
Paul was inducted into the Hall of Fame at Bloomfield Road, when it
was officially opened by Blackpool and England legend Jimmy Armfield in
April 2006. Organised by the Blackpool Supporters Association, Blackpool
fans around the world voted on their all-time heroes. Five players from
each decade were inducted; Stewart is in the 1980s.

THANKS

As stated previously, I had never intended to write a book but circumstances changed that decision in November 2016 when the football abuse scandal broke. In telling my story I met a reporter from the *Daily Mirror*, Jeremy Armstrong.

His patience and understanding of what was a very difficult subject matter was apparent from the start. I instantly saw a quality in him that you don't often get within his industry, therefore when I decided to tell my story, he became my natural choice as a ghostwriter.

I would like to take this opportunity to thank him not only for the manner in which he has handled the nature of the story, but his professionalism and the unrelenting effort that has been involved in writing this book, the countless hours we have spent, so as to make sure this book reflects exactly how the abuse has impacted on my life, and the hard work in bringing my voice through within the story.

Jeremy I am indebted to you for life, and I am honoured to call you my friend. Thank you.

To my mum and dad and two older brothers, Gary and Anthony, thank you for all your help over the past year. I know it must have been as difficult for you as it has been for me. I love you all dearly.

ACKNOWLEDGEMENTS

Thanks also to all the managers, coaches and players that have said so many positive things from my times with them as a player, under some difficult circumstances, in particular to Sam Ellis, my former Blackpool manager, who has remained a close friend, and taught me the principles as a young player that I still adhere to, to this day.

Finally, I would like to thank Steve Hanrahan and Paul Dove at the publishers, Trinity Mirror Sport Media, for giving me the chance to tell my story.

Paul displayed relentless diligence in bringing the book to life, and has turned the hours of interviews into something that I can honestly say is true to how it really happened.

Thanks also to Rick Cooke for his design vision and expertise and photographer Tony Woolliscroft for his professionalism.

Above all, I'd like to finish by paying tribute to my wife Beverley and my three children Adam, Chloe and Jade for all their support and love. Without them, I wouldn't be here to tell the story.

Paul Stewart

SAFEGUARDING AND VICTIM ENGAGEMENT

4 footballers/15 years of childhood sexual abuse/
95 years in the game/100 years of non-disclosure

'SAVE', which stands for Safeguarding and Victim Engagement, was born in December 2016. It is an organisation that was set up by Paul Stewart, Ian Ackley, David White and Derek Bell.

The four of us met at Wembley having been invited to discuss the escalating 'historical childhood sexual abuse in football' issue that had engulfed the media.

Immediately it became clear, along with empathy with each other, we had common ground. We wanted to be part of the solution, not a distraction to it.

The meeting with the FA was successful. After many more such meetings and telephone calls it became abundantly clear that we were making a difference and were in a unique and maybe privileged position to be an integral part of the solution, the way forward.

We particularly thank Greg Clarke and Sue Ravenlaw at the FA, Gordon Taylor and Darren Wilson at the PFA, Colin Bland at Sporting Chance and Doctor Elly Hanson for all their co-operation, collaboration and assistance to this point and no doubt moving forward.

David, Derek, Ian & Paul

SAVE
SAFEGUARDING AND VICTIM ENGAGEMENT

The Philosophy

- We will be transparent
- We will collaborate
- We will share information
- We will not step on others' toes
- We will not default to criticism
- We will be honest
- We will work with integrity
- We will be clear about our positions
- We will not work beyond our skillset

So far, Save has...

- Developed a healthy, colloborative approach with the FA
- Been influential in the development of the victims' support package in football alongside the FA, the PFA, Sporting Chance and Doctor Elly Hanson
- Met with and liaised with representatives of Operation Hydrant in an effort to understand their aims, power and difficulties
- Worked with the FA to develop research regarding the overall understanding of 'safeguarding' at grassroots level
- Liaised with fellow victims, advised, signposted and 'walked with them to the next place' in their recovery
- Presented our thoughts to both the Premier League and the English Football League

SAFEGUARDING/VICTIM ENGAGEMENT

Our areas of involvement

• Mandarory reporting:
• Criminal record checks
• Incident reporting protocol
• Induction and parental engagement
• Evidence-based club rating
• Unaffiliated junior football
• Education and accreditation
• Victim support
• Victim engagement

Contacts

www.saveassociation.com
enquiries@saveassociation.com
support@saveassociation.com

Telephone enquiries – 0330 043 0401
Telephone support – 0330 043 0701

facebook.com/saveassociation
twitter.com/saveassociation
instagram.com/saveassociation

4 footballers/15 years of childhood sexual abuse/
95 years in the game/100 years of non-disclosure/
less than 1 year together/a whole lot of progress/
1 positive future